MW01196361

LEXIS

LEXIS

ACADEMIC VOCABULARY STUDY

Arline Burgmeier

California State University, Fullerton

Gerry Eldred

Long Beach City College

Cheryl Boyd Zimmerman

California State University, Fullerton

Prentice Hall Regents
Englewood Cliffs, New Jersey 07632

Library of Congress Cataloging-in-Publication Data

Burgmeier, Arline, 1936–
    LEXIS : academic vocabulary study / Arline Burgmeier, Gerry
Eldred, Cheryl Boyd Zimmerman.
      p. cm.
    Includes index.
    ISBN 0-13-535022-0
    1. English language — Textbooks for foreign speakers.
2. Vocabulary. I. Eldred, Gerry, 1940–   . II. Zimmerman, Cheryl
Boyd, 1950–   . III. Title.
PE1128.B847 1991
428.2′4—dc20   90-46728
                                                       CIP

Editorial/production supervision: *Janet S. Johnston*
Manufacturing buyers: *Ray Keating, Lori Bulwin*
Cover design: *Miriam Recio*
Illustrations: *Kristen Burgmeier*
Copyreader: *Elaine Burgmeier*

 ©1991 by Prentice-Hall, Inc.
A Division of Simon & Schuster
Englewood Cliffs, New Jersey 07632

All rights reserved. No part of this book may be reproduced,
in any form or by any means, without permission in writing from
the publisher.

10   9   8   7   6   5   4   3   2   1

ISBN 0-13-535022-0

Prentice-Hall International (UK) Limited, *London*
Prentice-Hall of Australia Pty. Limited, *Sydney*
Prentice-Hall Canada Inc., *Toronto*
Prentice-Hall Hispanoamericana, S.A., *Mexico*
Prentice-Hall of India Private Limited, *New Delhi*
Prentice-Hall of Japan, Inc., *Tokyo*
Simon & Schuster Asia Pte. Ltd., *Singapore*
Editora Prentice-Hall do Brasil, Ltda., *Rio de Janeiro*

CONTENTS

PREFACE

Lexis: Academic Vocabulary Study helps students acquire the large and accurate vocabulary they need for academic success. Designed for high-intermediate ESL classes or developmental English classes, *Lexis* presents a wide variety of communicative activities that expand students' language skills through intensive practice with high-frequency academic vocabulary.

Unlike other vocabulary texts that focus merely on building the passive vocabulary, *Lexis* focuses on increasing the students' active vocabulary so that they learn not only the meaning of words but also their use in original expression.

At the beginning of each chapter, students encounter target words in the meaningful context of a high-interest reading selection. In the succeeding activities they must recognize the words in different but related contexts. At the same time they are given practice with word formation skills that will help them recognize and understand new words that they encounter. Students also learn to utilize the dictionary as a vocabulary-expanding tool. Subsequent activities allow students to use the words in natural communicative situations. Through this process, students are able to take an unfamiliar word, incorporate it first into their passive vocabularies, then ultimately into their active vocabularies. The book affords practice in all four language skills (reading, writing, listening, and speaking) to give students extensive practice with the words they are learning.

To give students a thorough understanding of the target words and their usage, *Lexis* approaches vocabulary study on three levels: the word level, the sentence level, and the context level. The organization of each chapter reflects this approach.

Establishing a Context

Each chapter begins with pre-reading questions that focus the students' mind-set on a particular context that will become the theme of the chapter. The context itself is a 1500-to-2000 word article on a high-interest topic related to such academic disciplines as business, psychology, language, history, and biology. Comprehension questions about the article check the students' understanding of what they have read.

Understanding Words

Students are presented a list of approximately 40 vocabulary words taken from the article. These words have been singled out because they are high-frequency words that are broadly applicable in university-level general education courses. Technical and idiomatic words have been avoided because they tend to have limited application. Initial activities focus on establishing the general meaning of each word as it is used in the article. Other activities at the word level are designed to familiarize students with decoding devices that will help them understand the meaning and function of new words they encounter, and encoding devices that will enable them to create new forms of words they learn. These devices include the use of prefixes and suffixes, capitalization, and pluralization.

Putting Words into Sentences

Ten words are selected from the original vocabulary list for further study. These words have multiple meanings and multiple forms. Vocabulary-expanding activities teach students related forms of target words and give semantic and syntactic information about them so that students can use them confidently in sentences. Numerous activities give students the opportunity to use the words in natural contexts. Finally, sociocultural information that may affect word usage helps students learn to use the words appropriately. The text avoids manipulative exercises and instead includes cognitive activities that encourage students to consider sentence meaning as well as form. Activities are contextualized according to the theme of the chapter, enabling students to learn not only new words but facts related to the theme. Sentence-level activities focus on formations such as paraphrasing, passivization, comparatives and superlatives, and collocations.

Using Words in Context

Just as words do not occur in isolation, but within the context of a sentence, neither do sentences occur in isolation, but within the context of a larger discourse. This section focuses on semantic, syntactic, and rhetorical devices, such as text integration, paraphrasing, and summarizing, that transcend sentence boundaries. Finally, students are asked to demonstrate their mastery of the target words in a variety of oral and written activities that require original expression.

Although each chapter is independent, vocabulary words from earlier chapters are recycled in subsequent readings and activities. To maximize the benefit of recycling, chapters should be studied in the order given. The abundance of activities permits the teacher to select those which best fit the class time frame. It also frees the teacher from the chore of making up supplementary exercises and quizzes. Activities are designed to allow flexibility and can be done as written homework or as oral communicative classwork. An alphabetized word list at the back of the book is a convenient index for locating vocabulary words included in the text. A selected glossary helps explain grammatical and linguistic terms.

Lexis is sufficiently rich in content to serve as the main text in a language classroom. Its three-level approach to vocabulary acquisition and its stress on elevating words to the active vocabulary set *Lexis* apart from other vocabulary texts.

1

LANGUAGE CHANGE AND THE DEVELOPMENT OF AMERICAN ENGLISH

ESTABLISHING A CONTEXT

Pre-reading Discussion

- When you don't know the meaning of a word, how do you find out what it means?
- Why do so many words in English have similar meanings?
- Why do the British say *lift* and the Americans say *elevator* when they mean the same thing?
- What does the title of this book—*Lexis*—mean?

> Read this article for general meaning. If you cannot understand the meaning of the content, use a dictionary to look up key words (words that are important to the meaning).

(1) Language is the system of communication through which humans send messages. Scholars theorize that the earliest language came into existence 80,000 years ago when humans used hand signals to communicate while hunting to avoid scaring off the hunted animal. These scholars also believe that the use of gestures evolved into a form of vocalization with sounds symbolizing specific gestures.

(2) It is unknown how humans invented words, but educated guesses can be made as to the reasons they did. These reasons include identifying people in their groups, naming objects, such as animals and plants, expressing the ideas of time, and communicating needs such as ''I am hungry.''

(3) Humans gradually built a storehouse of language symbols that represented objects and actions in the outside world. As civilization progressed, language changed to reflect new knowledge and a more complex society. Language continued to change throughout time for a variety of reasons.

(4) How a language evolves can be traced in the development of the English language and what came to be the American language. An early dialect of English was brought to England at the beginning of the 5th century by wandering Germanic tribes

called Angles, Saxons, and Jutes. The language of that period, now called Anglo-Saxon or Old English, became the basis of the English language. Hundreds of common words still in use today have their roots in Anglo-Saxon. Examples include *man, wife, child, house, good, strong, full, bones, big, king,* and *queen.* Later when Scandinavian tribes conquered England, they contributed words like *husband, call, gate, egg,* and many other common words. When Christianity was brought to England, many church-related Latin words were added to Anglo-Saxon, such as *candle, shrine, priest, monk, angel,* and *sabbath.* Latin also added such everyday words as *cap, cook, school,* and *circle.* Later classic literary works of the Romans and Greeks contributed such words as *bonus, logic, pedestrian,* and *diagram.*

(5)   Although the Scandinavian and Latin influences on the English language were great, the most significant foreign influence on English came from French after the French-Norman occupation of England in 1066. In the years that followed, thousands of French words were added to the English language. While English dominated as the language of the common people, the language of the ruling upper class was French. Therefore, it is not surprising that many of the newly added words reflected the superior position of the upper class: *government, tax, judge, prison, soldier, battle,* and *guard* are just a few. Others are *luxury, gown, jewel, diamond, chair, leisure, dance, music, marriage, medicine,* and *physician.*

(6)   The foreign influences on English, particularly the influence of French, are responsible for the richness of synonymous words in English. *Smell* and *stench,* for example, were supplemented by French words like *aroma, odor, scent, perfume,* and *fragrance.* Still more synonyms come from Latin, and their tone is often more "bookish" than those of English and French. In the following sets of words, the first is English, the second French, and the third Latin: *ask/question/interrogate, fast/firm/secure, fear/terror/trepidation,* and *time/age/epoch.*

(7)   The French-Norman conquest not only led to the addition of thousands of new words to the English language, but it also influenced existing English words. An example of the French influence on English can be seen in the spelling and pronunciation changes of the Anglo-Saxon word *house.* The Old English word was spelled *hus* and pronounced [ho͞os]; the French changed the spelling to *hous.* In the Middle English period, the spelling became *house,* possibly to reflect the pronunciation of the final *e* at that time [housə]. Today the word is spelled with a final *e* even though that letter is no longer pronounced.

(8)   The fact that English spelling is not always in harmony with English pronunciation can be partially explained by describing language changes. Historically, the sounds within some words have changed, but the spelling of these words has not. For example, in Chaucer's time (late 14th century), the word *name* would have been pronounced [nămə]. In Shakespeare's time (1564–1616), *seam* was pronunced [sām] and did not rhyme with *dream,* as it does now. The *k* in *knife* was pronounced, as were the *g* in *gnaw* and *-gh* in *night.* Another reason for the inconsistency between the spelling and pronunciation of English is related to the invention of the printing press in England around 1476. The printed forms of the word tended to be standardized, while the pronunciation varied and continued to change.

A 19th-century eight-cylinder type-revolving printing press. Courtesy of the New York Public Library Picture Collection.

(9)   Language change also helps account for irregular forms in English, such as some plurals, like *children* and *mice*, and past tense verb forms, like *bought* and *went*. The past tense of many common verbs of Old English was indicated by vowel change, such as *sing/sang*, *drive/drove*, and *get/got*, rather than by adding the standard past tense suffix *-ed* as in *walk/walked*. Many of these verbs have retained their old forms to this day. We now consider them ''irregular'' verbs.

(10)   American English had its beginning when Great Britain colonized America in the 17th century. Although 90 percent of the population were descendants of British colonists, settlers from other countries made the nation a multilingual society much like it is today.

(11)   As the new nation grew and the pioneers settled their new land, the American language developed. Many words were borrowed from the languages of the native Indians to describe natural objects that had no counterparts in England. Examples included the names of animals: *raccoon*, *opossum*, and *moose*. In addition to the Indian words, words were adopted from other languages, such as *pretzel*, *spook*, *depot*, and *canyon* from German, Dutch, French, and Spanish, respectively. Early American settlers made up words that were added to the language, such as *lengthy*, *calculate*, *seaboard*, *bookstore*, and *presidential*. Thomas Jefferson, the drafter of the Declaration of Independence, invented the word *belittle*, and in his time the words *cent* and *dollar* were added to American English.

(12)   Over time, differences in pronunciation, spelling, vocabulary, and grammar developed between British and American English. A spirit of independence that followed the American Revolution was accompanied by the desire to form a language that was separate from British English. As a result, Americans such as Benjamin Franklin

and Noah Webster made it a personal crusade to reform the American English spelling system. Thus, we now have spelling differences such as *color* for the British *colour, wagon* for *waggon, defense* for *defence, honor* for *honour, theater* for *theatre,* and *tire* for *tyre.*

(13)   As a champion of American English, Webster attempted to standardize the pronunciation and spelling of American English by writing the first American dictionary. Until then there had been a tendency to spell words as they were spoken, such as "sartinly" (certainly) and "byled" (boiled), and to spell them differently in different regions. Webster's influence helped overcome the inconsistencies of spelling and pronunciation in America.

(14)   As English changes, dictionaries reflect the changes. Not only do words change in meaning, but new words are constantly added to a language. The enormous growth of English is reflected in the 315,000 entries in the 1988 edition of *Random House Dictionary,* 50,000 more than in the 1966 edition. Most new words today come from science and technology. Words that deal with computers such as *printout, software, input,* and *high-tech* have been added. American business and advertising have influenced the vocabulary, especially with brand names (like Coca-Cola and Kleenex, which have become generic terms for *cola* and *tissue*). Politics has made an impact on the language: the suffix -*gate,* which came from Watergate in the Nixon era, has become associated with political scandal. Even the language of adolescents has influenced dictionary entries. Old words like *punk, cool,* and *boss,* for example, have been given new meanings.

(15)   Modern English is still expanding by borrowing words from other languages. Americans run *marathons,* learn *algebra,* sleep in *pajamas,* live in *patio* homes, and eat in *sushi* bars or at *smorgasbord* buffets. Just as English has borrowed many words from other languages, many English words have been borrowed by other countries. French now has *le drugstore, le weekend,* and *le playboy.* Germans wear *die Jeans* and listen to *die soundtrack.* In Hong Kong, dancers visit a *dixie-go.* The Japanese have formed new words like *man-shon* (condominium), *mai-kaa,* and *mai-town.*

(16)   English has become a global language, used in communications, in technical and scientific journals, and in technology. In fact, nearly 80 percent of the information stored in the world's computers is in English. English, the official language of the Olympics, is used internationally in sports, in beauty contests, in transportation (airlines and ships), and in religious and secular broadcasting.

(17)   As the United States continues its tradition of being a society of mixed cultures, American English will continue to change as the world around us changes.

Comprehension Check

The purpose of this activity is to check your understanding of the article and to give practice using vocabulary words. Label each sentence true or false according to the article. If you cannot understand the meaning of a sentence, use a dictionary to look up key words.

1. Scientists theorize that language evolved as early humans used sounds to symbolize objects, people, and needs.
2. Language change can reflect knowledge that is added to the human storehouse of information.
3. When the French-Normans conquered England, English became the language of the ruling class.
4. The Greeks contributed many words to the English language, especially in the areas of government, schools, and church.
5. As French words supplemented the English language, a richness of synonyms resulted.
6. Thomas Jefferson started a crusade to reform the spelling system of American English.
7. Early Americans adopted the Indian names for animals that had no counterparts in England.
8. The inconsistency between spelling and pronunciation can be partially explained by the fact that the spoken word evolved constantly, while the printed language remained more fixed.
9. The tendency to change brand-name products into generic words accounts for new words like *Kleenex*.
10. English vocabulary has constantly expanded as a result of the impact made by a multilingual population.

UNDERSTANDING WORDS

Vocabulary List

Verbs		Nouns	Adjectives/Participles	Adverbials
account (for)	occupy	counterpart	classic	constantly
conquer	progress	crusade	enormous	partially
consider	reflect	descendant	generic	respectively
contribute	reform	impact		
deal (with)	represent	inconsistency		
dominate	supplement	richness		
evolve	symbolize	tendency		
expand	theorize			
form	trace			

Subject-Specific Vocabulary

Nouns: dialect, suffix, synonym.   **Adjective:** multilingual.

This book will help you learn specific words and will also help you become a word learner. People learn a word in two general ways: through experience and through the use of a dictionary. In this book you will learn the new words by using them repeatedly in a variety of activities. The book will also give you practice using the dictionary to clarify word meanings.

When you read a word you do not know, follow these steps:

1. Ask yourself if you really need to know the word in order to understand the sentence. In which of the following sentences is the meaning of the underlined word important to the general meaning of the sentence?

> The little boy sat under a banyan tree, dreaming of the day when he would be big enough to work with the men.
> Benjamin Franklin was known for his frugality.

In the first sentence, the main idea concerns the little boy's thoughts about the future. Where he was sitting is not critical to the meaning of the sentence, so you can understand the sentence without knowing the details about a banyan tree. In the second sentence, frugality contains the main idea of the sentence. Without it you do not know what Benjamin Franklin is known for.

2. If you do need to know the word, look for context clues. Following are five different kinds of context clues that will help you guess the meaning of the words.

   a. Synonym or restatement clues
      It is difficult to find a pristine, or unspoiled, forest in the United States.

   b. Comparison or contrast clues
      Although Harold is very loquacious, his wife is very quiet.

   c. Example clues
      The student procrastinated starting his homework. He washed his car, telephoned a friend, watched television, and finally started studying at midnight.

   d. Experience or situation clues
      The young woman packed her clothes in a valise and hurried to the airport.

   e. Direct explanation or summary clues
      The computer science student was successful because of his tenacity; that is, he was determined to understand how to write a program, and he continued to work until he wrote one successfully.

3. If you can't guess the meaning of the word from the context, look at the word itself and see if you can break it into parts that have meaning. For example:

   im polite ness   re occur ence

4. If you still don't know the word, look it up in the dictionary.

Activity 1

Read each sentence or group of sentences carefully. Then use the context clues to guess the meaning of the underlined word.

1. Switzerland is a multilingual nation. Its residents speak French, German, and Italian.
2. Alaska is an enormous state. Rhode Island, on the other hand, is very small.
3. Since the American flag is meant to symbolize, or represent, the unity and the history of the nation, it is displayed in front of government buildings.
4. Shakespeare's plays have had lasting significance and value in the world of literature. Such classics are greatly valued by English-speaking people.
5. The rich family contributed two million dollars to the museum.
6. The governor wants to keep the university scholarship program the same as it has been for fifty years, but his opponents are hoping to reform it.
7. George Washington and his wife had no children, so this famous president had no descendants.

Activity 2

A word can have several meanings. You have to look at the way the word is used in a sentence in order to understand its meaning. Often you will find clues to the meaning in the original sentence or in surrounding sentences. Study this example.

> The creator of the atom bomb **reflected** on, or thought about, the effect it would have on humans and the future of the world.

The words "thought about" tell what *reflected* means. This is a context clue. In the following sentences, identify the clues that help you understand the use of *reflect*.

1. The child saw her face reflected in the mirror.
2. Language reflects change in society. For example, computer-related words recently added to the language show the importance of computers.
3. Some people think that the behavior of a child reflects on the parents. If the child behaves badly, the parents are to blame or are responsible.
4. Light colors reflect heat, but dark colors absorb heat instead of throwing it back.

Activity 3

Sometimes knowing the meaning of parts of words will help you understand the word without looking in the dictionary. For example the prefix *pre-* at the beginning of a word often means "before." *Re-* means "again." What do the underlined words mean in these sentences?

1. The manager attended a premeeting luncheon.
2. Halley's Comet reappears approximately every 75 years.

3. Many people have tried to <u>reform</u> the English spelling system.

4. People who <u>prepay</u> their hotel bills may get a discount.

The prefix *counter-* has several meanings. Look for this prefix in your dictionary, then tell what the underlined words mean.

5. The U.S. president met with his British <u>counterpart</u> to discuss a new trade agreement.

6. The dancers moved <u>counterclockwise</u> around the room.

7. Aware that he was losing the game, the brilliant chess player planned a clever <u>counterattack</u>.

Activity 4

If you are unable to find a certain word in the dictionary, breaking the word into parts may help you find it. The main part of the word is called the "root" or "base." A part added before the base is a prefix, and a part added after the base is a suffix. For example:

preoccupation   (pre   + occupy + ation)
           prefix + base   + suffix

A word with a prefix or a suffix may sometimes be found as a main entry in a dictionary, or it may be found with the entry for the base word. For example, the word *prepay* may not be in the dictionary, so look for *pay*. The words *greatness* and *liveliness* can be found under *great* and *lively*, respectively. Thus, words with suffixes such as -able, -er, -less, -like, -ly, and -ation may be found in a dictionary under the base word entry.

Look up these words in your dictionary. If a word does not appear as a main entry, where can you find it?

unrepresentative	disregard	lifelike	sensationally
progressively	indigestible	multilingual	unforeseeable
conqueror	inconsistency	realistic	visionary

Activity 5

Words that are similar in meaning are synonyms, and those that are opposite in meaning are antonyms. To understand the meaning of a word, sometimes it helps to know its opposite. Which of the following pairs of words are antonyms, and which are synonyms?

tendency/likelihood	constantly/seldomly	counterpart/opposite
expand/contract	partially/completely	multilingual/monolingual
occupy/inhabit	supplement/add to	consistency/inconsistency
trace/follow		

Activity 6

Which word or group of words has the same meaning as the underlined word in each sentence?

1. The committee chairman had to account for how the money was spent.

    explain   decide   add up   find out

2. America as a union of 50 states expanded from the colonies along the Atlantic Coast.

    governed   changed   grew   started

3. A new language, "computerese" or "computer talk," was formed with the development of the personal computer.

    used   created   spoken   written

4. To many immigrants, the Statue of Liberty symbolizes freedom.

    leads to   helps   lives in   represents

5. Scientists theorize that humans are descendants of apes.

    explain   believe   argue   prove

6. Some psychologists believe that television has an impact on children, mostly negative.

    understanding   outcome   effect   interest

7. The majority party got the most votes; respectively, the conservative candidate got 40 percent, and the radical candidate got 60 percent.

    surprisingly   only   easily   individually

8. She carefully considered the matter before she made the decision to marry the prince.

    talked about   described   learned about   thought about

Activity 7

Main entries in a dictionary may have more than one part of speech, for example, adjective (**ADJ**), noun (**N**), verb (**V**), adverb (**ADV**), preposition (**PREP**). Identify the underlined words below as nouns, verbs, adjectives, or adverbials.

1. He stopped the car suddenly.
2. She jumped higher than ever before.
3. You look nice in your new suit.
4. The student's progress was impressive.
5. They considered the options carefully.
6. To apply for the college, I had to fill out many forms.
7. The project is progressing on schedule.
8. My friend always dominates the conversation.

9. The Christians <u>led</u> a <u>crusade</u> to <u>expand</u> their religion.
10. People often <u>supplement</u> their <u>diets</u> with vitamin pills.
11. The detective <u>traced</u> the criminal's activities to the <u>source</u> of the crime.
12. The police <u>chief</u> <u>crusaded</u> against crime.

Activity 8

In a dictionary, verbs may be identified as **VT** or **VI**. **VT** means "verb transitive"—the verb must be followed by an object. **VI** means "verb intransitive"—no object is used after the verb. Some verbs may be either transitive or intransitive. Look at the following sentences. (For an explanation of what the symbols **S**, **V**, and **O** represent, see the glossary at the end of the book.)

        S   **V**   **O**
The horse carried a rider.   (*Carry* is always transitive.)

        S   **V**
The horse slept standing up.   (*Sleep* is always intransitive.)

        S   **V**   **O**
The horse kicked the barn door.

        S   **V**   (*Kick* is transitive or intransitive.)
The horse kicked violently.

Read each sentence below. If the verb is transitive, add an object after the verb. If the verb is intransitive, add nothing. If the verb is both transitive and intransitive, write it or say it both ways. For example, *speak* can be both transitive and intransitive.

She spoke _____ *with a slight accent.*
She spoke English with a slight accent.
She spoke with a slight accent.

1. Many languages have contributed _____ to the English language.

2. People learning English as a second language may have difficulty dealing with _____ at first.

3. Like English, other languages have evolved _____ over many centuries.

4. The Angles, Saxons, and Jutes occupied _____ hundreds of years ago.

5. H_2O symbolizes _____ in chemistry.

6. The Normans conquered _____ in 1066.

7. Americans consider _____ difficult to learn.

8. Lexicographers can trace _____ to their earlier forms.

9. Musicians constantly practice _____.

Activity 9

Words that are the same in spelling but are different in meaning and origin are often listed as separate entries in a dictionary. An entry may have several definitions. For example:

> **deal**¹ *vt.* dealt, dealing **1.** to give out or distribute **2.** to administer, give or deliver   *n.* **1.** the giving out of cards in a card game **2.** a business arrangement or transaction   Colloq.* treatment—good or bad [a fair deal, a dirty deal]
> **deal**² *n.* a quantity or degree of something, usually a large amount
> **deal with** *vi.* **1.** to do business with someone or trade in something **2.** to be about something (subject matter) **3.** to behave in a certain way toward others
> **reform**¹ *vt.* **1.** to cause to improve, make better or right   *vi.* to improve one's behavior
> **reform**² *vt.* to form again

In the sentences below, write the entry that reflects the meaning of the underlined words. The first one has been done for you.

1. The college student had a great <u>deal</u> of trouble with his calculus class.

   <u>a large amount</u>

2. The study of linguistics <u>deals</u> with the history of language and language change. _____

3. The two companies made a <u>deal</u> to exchange manufacturing methods.

   _____

4. It takes patience to <u>deal</u> with small children. _____

5. In England, numerous attempts were made to <u>reform</u> the spelling system.

   _____

6. The potter disliked the first shape of the bowl, so he <u>reformed</u> it.

   _____

7. After the prisoner was released, he promised to <u>reform</u>.

   _____

Activity 10

Look up the following underlined words in your dictionary and write the definition that fits the meaning of the word as it is used in the sentence.

1. They <u>conquered</u> their fear of flying by participating in group therapy.
2. The Incas of Peru were <u>conquered</u> by the Spaniards.

*For an explanation of colloq., see **colloquialism** in the glossary.

3. As the western frontier in America expanded, the American language changed, adding new words that <u>reflected</u> the new environment.

4. Iron <u>expands</u> when it is heated.

5. The English language was influenced by the various nations that <u>occupied</u> England prior to the 12th century.

6. The student had little free time because he was <u>occupied</u> with his homework.

7. My office seems crowded because the books <u>occupy</u> so much space.

8. I couldn't stay at the hotel because all of the rooms were <u>occupied</u>.

9. He didn't seem to understand me. I think he was mentally <u>preoccupied</u>.

Activity 11

Which of the following meanings for *contribute* fit the sentences below?

    1. to share or participate in; to give something
    2. to write an article, as for a magazine
    3. to furnish ideas
    4. to help in bringing about

_____ Norman Vincent Peale contributes a column in several newspapers.

_____ Cigarette smoking contributed to his poor health.

_____ We all contributed money to the Emergency Relief Fund.

_____ Each member of the discussion group contributed.

Activity 12

Rich and *wealthy* are synonyms and are interchangeable. *Richness* and *wealth* have similar meanings but are not always interchangeable. When referring to money, only *wealth* can be used, but when referring to the quality of something, either can be used.

    In which sentences below is *richness* correctly used? In sentences where it is incorrectly used, make the sentence correct.

1. Butter added to the richness of the cake.

2. The richness of the soil was apparent in its dark color.

3. The richness of the king was evident from his jewels.

4. I liked the fabric because of its richness.

5. His fancy car was a symbol of his richness.

Activity 13

A *dialect* is a variety of a language spoken in different parts of a country or in another country, such as British English and American English. Words from the same language are often pronounced differently by region or country, and there may be differences in vocabulary use. For example, look in your dictionary for the pronunciation of *aunt*. Which pronunciation do you hear where you live?

Some dictionaries list British and American spellings of the same word. See if these British words are in your dictionary. What is the American counterpart of each?

lift (noun)	flat (noun)	theatre	cheque
lorry	bonnet (car part)	colour	defence

Activity 14

Look up the word *classic* in your dictionary. Tell what the word means in each of these sentences and whether it is being used as a noun or an adjective.

1. Michelangelo was an architect and poet, but he is best known as a classic painter and sculptor.
2. Elizabeth is a graduate student in English, specializing in the classics.
3. *Gone with the Wind* is an American classic in literature and in cinema.
4. Gary's 1955 Porsche is valued as a classic by car collectors.
5. Oscar De La Renta has consistently designed clothes in a classic style.
6. Bob Hope is a classic example of a comedian.

Activity 15

The noun form of *enormous* is *enormity*. Some synonyms for *enormous* are *gigantic, monstrous, huge,* and *vast*. What are the noun forms for these words?

> Humongus is a slang word that has been formed by combining huge and monstrous.

Activity 16

Constantly refers to doing something without stopping or doing something frequently over an extended period of time. Which of the following do you do constantly?

make spelling mistakes	forget to pay bills
smoke too much	bite your fingernails
drive too fast	diet

Activity 17

Which of the statements below are only partially true, according to the article?

1. Benjamin Franklin and Noah Webster were champions of language reform in early America.
2. French, German, Latin, and Chinese have all contributed enormously to the English language.

3. American English adopted words such as man, wife, and house from the native Indian languages.

4. Some English verbs resisted change; they are now considered regular verbs.

Activity 18

Xerox has become a generic term for photocopying.

I have to xerox some papers.

Some brand names are so closely associated with a certain type of product that the brand name becomes a generic or common term for all similar products. Match the product on the right with the generic, or common, term on the left.

1. zipper
2. aspirin
3. Kleenex
4. Levis
5. Coca-Cola
6. Jello

a. a drug for headaches
b. a soft drink
c. denim pants
d. a facial tissue
e. gelatin
f. a fastener on pants or jackets

Activity 19

The title of this book, *Lexis*, is a Greek word. Look in your dictionary for the origin of the word—its etymology. If you can't find it as a main entry, what can you look under? What does it mean? What do these words mean?

lexicon   lexicography   lexicographer

Activity 20

Discuss the following questions in pairs or small groups.

1. What language dominates in each of these countries?
   Brazil   Canada   Panama   the Philippines   Vietnam   India

2. The prefix *multi-* means "many." What does it mean if a person is a multimillionaire? What if a business is multinational?

3. What do these represent?

   1. A.D.
   2. B.C.
   3. A.M.
   4. M.A.
   5. Ph.D
   6. M.D.
   7. RSVP
   8. IOU
   9. c/o
   10. etc.
   11. i.e.
   12. e.g.

4. If two things or actions are inconsistent with each other, they are not in harmony or agreement. Which of the following actions represent an inconsistency in behavior?
   a. dieting/eating donuts for breakfast
   b. being a good student/studying daily
   c. opposing the use of hand guns/going hunting with rifles
   d. having a concern for the environment/recycling aluminum cans

5. Some people have a tendency to behave in a certain way. For example, teenagers have a tendency to drive too fast. What are some things that these people have a tendency to do?

politicians	senior citizens
English teachers	first-year college students
men	car salesmen
women	actresses

6. Which of the following can expand in size? Which can decrease or contract?

heated iron	a waistline	cooling metal
a balloon	a melting ice cube	a rubber band
population	a bank account	

7. Match the item on the right with its counterpart on the left.

king	abacus
castle	clock
calculator	prime minister
sundial	mansion
president	queen

PUTTING WORDS INTO SENTENCES

Ten words have been selected from the original vocabulary list for closer study. These words and their related forms are listed below.

Verbs	Nouns	Adjectives/ Participles	Adverbials
account for	account	accountable	
conquer	conquest conqueror	conquered	
dominate	domination dominance	dominant	dominantly
predominate	predominance	predominant	predominantly
evolve	evolution	evolutionary	
form	form	formative	
formulate	formation		
occupy	occupation	(un)occupied preoccupied	
progress	progress	progressive	progressively
reflect	reflection	reflective reflected	reflectively
represent	representation representative	(un)representative	
symbolize	symbol symbolism	symbolic	symbolically

Activity 1

To account for means "to give an explanation or reason for something."

> *A businessman must account for his expenses while traveling for his company.*
> *The accused thief couldn't account for his time on the day of the bank robbery.*

Practice using *account for* in written sentences that combine the following word groups:

corporation president/sales drop
bookkeeper/$1,000 shortage
car manufacturer/faulty gear shifts
on new cars

student/absences from class
child/mother/lost sweater

On account of means "because of."
> The schools were closed on account of the holiday.

By all accounts means "according to what everyone says."
> By all accounts, English is a difficult language to learn.

To take into account means "to consider or to think about."
> In deciding which person to hire, the employer took into account each person's experience.

Activity 2

If a person is accountable for an action, then that person is responsible for the action.

> *The president is accountable for actions that affect the public.*

Combine the information on the right with the appropriate person on the left, using *to be accountable for* in your sentences.

1. teachers
2. parents
3. industrialists
4. commercial pilots

clean environment
students' achievements
safety of passengers
children's behavior

In a sentence that tells who requires the responsibility, the phrase "to hold accountable for" can be used.

> *The voters hold the president accountable for decisions that affect the public.*

Using the above list, tell who holds the people on the left accountable.

Activity 3

To dominate has several meanings. One is "to have or exercise controlling power." *Dominance* means "importance, power, or controlling influence."

> Read the following paragraph.

(a) Mexico, like other Latin American countries, was a nation greatly influenced by foreign conquest. (b) The original inhabitants of Mexico were Indians of various tribes, the Aztecs being a dominant tribe. (c) The Spanish conqueror, Hernando Cortes, brought about the downfall of a strong civilization, which was followed by the dominance of the Spanish culture, especially in its language and customs. (d) Even though the conquered natives adopted the Spanish language, many of their Indian customs have been maintained to this day.

Restate the numbered sentences, using the words given. You may need to add words or change the word order to make the sentences logical and grammatical.

1. (Sentence **a**) conquerors . . . influenced Mexico
2. (Sentence **b**) Aztecs dominated
3. (Sentence **c**) the conquest of . . . Spanish culture dominated
4. (Sentence **d**) were conquered

Activity 4

To *dominate* generally refers to power, and *to predominate* refers to both power and to numbers. Use the information in Table 1.1 to describe immigration patterns, using the words and phrases given.

Table 1.1 **Immigration to the United States by Country of Birth, 1971–1986 (in thousands)**

	1961–70	1971–80	1981–85	1986
Germany	200.0	66.0	34.5	7.1
Italy	206.7	130.1	17.8	3.1
United Kingdom	230.5	123.5	71.7	13.7
Korea	35.8	272.0	166.0	35.8
Philippines	101.5	360.2	221.2	52.6
Vietnam	4.6	179.7	234.8	30.0
Mexico	44.3	637.2	335.2	66.5

1. 1961–70/predominated
2. 1971–80/predominantly
3. 1981–85/predominance of
4. 1986/predominant

Activity 5

To *evolve* means to develop gradually over a period of time. A thing evolves from something simple or basic into something more complex. The idea of *evolution* is usually associated with something living—people, animals, or plants. It can be used figuratively, as in ''the evolution of the jet airplane.''

English evolved from a basic Germanic dialect into a complex language of many dialects.

Linguists believe that gestures evolved into words and sounds.

Look at the words and phrases below. First decide which evolves *from* something and which evolves *into* something else. Then write sentences in which you combine the words and phrases. In some cases they may be written two ways.

1. butterfly · caterpillar
2. politician's ideas · laws
3. gestures · sounds and words
4. large-frame computers · personal computers
5. cosmopolitan city · village

The Theory of Evolution is credited to Charles Darwin, a 19th-century naturalist, who believed that man evolved from an earlier form of life.

Activity 6

Read the following paragraph.

(a) A human being is a fascinating creature in that it evolves from a very small form of life. (b) Human life begins to form with the joining of the male sperm and the female ova. (c) The formation of a network of neurons is even more remarkable, resulting in the evolution of the brain.

Restate the numbered sentences, using the words given. You may need to add words or change the word order to make the sentences logical and grammatical.

1. (Sentence **a**) The evolutionary group . . . formation of
2. (Sentence **b**) The formative stages of life
3. (Sentence **c**) . . . is formed and evolves
4. (Sentence **c**) evolves

To formulate means "to express in a short clear form" or "to invent and prepare."

The professor formulates his ideas well.
Who formulated the plans for the space exploration?

Activity 7

Use the facts below to formulate sentences with the information and word forms given.

43 A.D.	Roman conquest of Britain
1066	Normans conquered Britain
until 1492	No foreigners had settled in America
after World War II	Foreign powers took over eastern European territories

1. occupied
2. occupation of
3. unoccupied
4. occupied territories

Activity 8

Progress suggests forward motion. Like any forward motion, it can be stopped, slowed or facilitated (made easier).

A lack of materials slowed the progress of the new building.

Restate the following sentences, using a form of *progress*. It can be used as a noun or a verb.

1. The student was improving his performance in mathematics.
2. The government provided more money to help advance medical research.
3. Bad weather slowed the advancement of the military troops.

Activity 9

Progressively means "over a period of time."

English changed as human knowledge became progressively more complex.

Notice that *progressively* is followed by a comparative form (*more complex*).

Answer the following questions, using *progressively* and the words in parentheses.

1. Why do people with fixed incomes have difficulty maintaining a standard of living? (more expensive)
2. How do you know if a fire engine is getting closer when you are driving along the street? (louder)
3. How do you know if a storm is developing in the sky? (darker)
4. Why would a doctor order a patient to enter a hospital? (worse)

> **To make progress** means "to make continual improvement or development."
> The patient was making progress after the accident. (He was getting better.)

Activity 10

Describe the progress made according to the test scores in Table 1.2, using the given forms of *progress* and where possible a descriptive adjective or adverb such as *considerable/considerably, good/well, great/greatly, significant/significantly, rapid/rapidly, slow/slowly, steady/steadily.*

Table 1.2 Test Scores

Student	Nov.	Jan.	Mar.	Apr.	June
Roger	60	65	70	75	80
Bill	70	80	85	95	100
Martha	80	85	85	87	90
Grace	75	75	75	75	75

1. Roger: progress (verb)
2. Bill: progressively
3. Martha: progress (noun)
4. Grace: progress (verb)

Activity 11

Use the information in Table 1.3 to describe migratory patterns, using the given words and phrases below.

Table 1.3 Traces of Early Humans and Migratory Patterns

Species	Location
Homo sapiens	Africa → Europe → Siberia → Western Hemisphere, via Bering Strait and Australia, by sea
Homo erectus	Africa → Java → China → southern Europe
Homo habilis	Africa only

1. *Homo sapiens*
2. *Homo erectus*
3. *Homo habilis*

progressively migrated
progressed from . . . to
occupied

> To be progressive means "to favor or to use new ideas."
> The school is progressive because it uses the most modern ideas.

Activity 12

Write sentences using the given forms of *reflect*. You may have to change the word order to make logical and grammatical sentences.

1. mirror/yourself/reflection
2. color white/heat/reflect
3. windshield/glare/reflected
4. politicians/lying/reflects on/credibility
5. cheating/reflection on/student's character

> Reflective can mean "deeply in thought."
> She appeared to be in a reflective mood.

Activity 13

To symbolize something and to represent something both mean "to stand for something." A symbol is an object that represents something.

> The dove symbolizes peace.

In chemistry or mathematics, a symbol can be a mark or a letter standing for a quality or a process.

> H_2O is the symbol for water.

Write sentences using the given forms of symbolize. You may have to change the word order to make logical and grammatical sentences.

1. Statue of Liberty/freedom/symbol of
2. ring/marriage/symbolize
3. $/symbol for/ _____
4. a crown/symbolically/royalty

Activity 14

To represent something can mean "to symbolize something" or "to be an example of something."

> The Beatles' music represents the music of the '60s.

Representation is "a likeness of."

> The abstract painting seemed to be a representation of real-life objects.

Representative means "typical."

> Queen Elizabeth's dialect is representative of the educated class in England.

Write sentences using the word groups below. You may have to change the word order to make logical and grammatical sentences.

1. Elvis Presley/represent/50s/rock and roll
2. hippies/long hair/dirty clothes/no shoes/representative of
3. generic terms/representative of/brand names

> Representative as a noun refers to a person, such as an elected official, who represents the people of the country, state, or city where he or she was elected. It can also be a person who is acting in place of a group or another person, such as a sales representative.

Activity 15

Read the paragraph below.

The American flag has thirteen stripes, which are red and white, and a field of 50 white stars on a blue background. The stripes are representative of the original colonies that were established when the Pilgrims came to America. The colors red, white, and blue stand for courage, liberty, and justice, respectively. The stars signify the fifty individual states of the United States. The American flag is one of the few flags that reflect the change in the size of a nation.

Answer the questions below, using the words in parentheses.

1. What do the stripes on the American Flag signify? (represent)
2. What do red, white, and blue stand for? (representative of)
3. What do the 50 stars stand for? (represented by)

USING WORDS IN CONTEXT

Activity 1

Your instructor will dictate a paragraph about new words in the English dictionary. After you have written the paragraph, work with a partner to fill in words you may have missed or to correct grammar and spelling. When you and your partner believe your paragraphs are correct, compare them to the one printed at the back of the book. Make any necessary corrections.

Activity 2

Put the sentences below in chronological order. Use transitional words or phrases if needed between the sentences to form a paragraph.

_____ 1. After 407 A.D., Angles, Saxons, and Jutes overran England and brought a Germanic dialect.

_____ 2. English was influenced by the conquest of foreign powers.

_____ 3. In 1066, the French occupied England.

_____ 4. As a result of foreign domination, there are many synonymous words in English that have been borrowed from other languages.

_____ 5. The dialect of the Roman soldiers had an impact on the English language.

_____ 6. First, Britain was conquered by the Romans in 43 A.D.

_____ 7. Consequently, the vocabulary was supplemented with many French words.

Activity 3

Read the following paragraph as many times as you can in three minutes. Then with your book closed, rewrite as much of the information as you can remember.

The earliest human activity in Mexico can be traced back 40,000 years. Humans evolved from hunters to food collectors. This period was followed by an agricultural period during which village life expanded. The formation of societies progressed for the next eight centuries, called the Classic period, which saw the development and expansion of the Indian civilization. During the Postclassic period, Aztec Indians dominated, and they formed a capital city where Mexico City now stands. Today tourists can visit many historical sights that represent the early stages of Mexican history.

Writing Activity

Using the facts below, write a paragraph in which you discuss the history of Mexico in terms of who or what groups of people conquered, occupied, or dominated the country at various periods of time.

1440–1469	Montezuma, fifth Aztec king, conquered the area surrounding Tenochtitlan (the capital of Mexico) and expanded his empire to the Gulf of Mexico
1519–1521	Spanish expeditions led by Hernando Cortes and Juan de Grijalva; Cortes conquered Aztec capital in 1521; expansion of Spanish rule to Guatemala and Honduras
1521–1530	Other areas occupied by Spanish explorers
1716	Occupation by Spanish government began
1808	Napoleon Bonaparte occupied Spain
1821	Mexicans won independence from Spain
1863	French troops under Napoleon III occupied Mexico City
1864	Maximilian made emperor of Mexico by Napoleon
1867	Mexican troops regained power; Maximilian executed; end of foreign domination

Identical twins (above) are virtually indistinguishable, while fraternal twins (below) are no more alike than ordinary siblings. Identical twins, Shanghai, courtesy Porterfield-Chickering/Photo Researchers. Fraternal twins courtesy Bruce Roberts/Photo Researchers.

2

A NEW INTEREST IN TWINS

ESTABLISHING A CONTEXT

Pre-reading Discussion

- Why do family members resemble each other?
- Do you know any twins? In what ways are they alike? In what ways are they different?
- What do you consider some of the good things about being a twin? What do you consider some of the problems?

> Read this article for general meaning. If you cannot understand the meaning of a sentence, use a dictionary to look up key words (words that are important to the meaning).

(1)   When a baby is born, family members and friends are happy and excited. But when twins are born, family members and friends—and even strangers—are fascinated as well. "Do they like the same things?" people want to know. "Which one is smarter?" "How can you tell them apart?" The birth of twins is a phenomenon of nature that causes immediate interest. Throughout history, however, this interest was not always positive. In the past, some cultures considered the birth of twins as unnatural or evil, and the mother and her babies were put to death. On the other hand, other cultures welcomed twins because twins were believed to possess supernatural magical powers. Today modern societies do not consider twins as either unnatural or supernatural, but twins do continue to fascinate people. Scientists, too, have developed a keen interest in twins. Through the study of twins, scientists hope to learn something about the roles of heredity and environment in shaping human lives.

(2)   Children inherit characteristics from their parents through genes, microscopic bits of protein that carry the genetic code of an individual. Each child receives half of his or her genes from the mother and half from the father. Since both parents contribute to a child's heredity, children tend to resemble both of their parents. Yet the number of genes is so great that it is virtually impossible for a brother and a sister to receive

25

exactly the same combination of genes from the mother and the father. Therefore, two brothers, two sisters, or a brother and a sister may resemble each other, but they cannot be identical to each other unless they are twins. Only twins can be identical, and only a certain type of twins.

(3)   There are two types of twins, fraternal twins and identical twins. Fraternal twins result when the mother's ovaries release two ova at the same time, and these are fertilized by two separate sperm from the father. Although the resulting babies grow together in the womb during the nine months of pregnancy and are born at the same time, genetically they are no more alike than ordinary siblings born from separate pregnancies. Like ordinary brothers and sisters, fraternal twins may or may not closely resemble each other. They may be of different sexes and have different facial features, different eye and hair coloring, and different physiques.

(4)   In contrast, identical twins result when a single fertilized ovum separates into two identical embryos during the first 14 days after fertilization. During pregnancy, the embryos develop into two identical babies. The babies are genetically identical because they inherited the same genes from the union of their mother's single egg and their father's single sperm. Identical twins look like Xerox copies of each other. Often, especially in their early months, they are indistinguishable, even to their parents. Many parents of identical twins admit that they aren't completely certain which twin is which, so they may deal with the problem by using an identification system to tell them apart. For example, they might paint the toenails of one twin, or always dress one twin a certain color and dress the other twin in another color. As the babies grow older, slight differences that help distinguish one twin from the other might become apparent. For instance, one twin might have a distinctive feature, such as a freckle, that the other twin lacks.

(5)   As they mature, identical twins may continue to look so much alike that their friends and teachers confuse them. Sometimes twins delight in fooling people by trading places with each other. And no wonder others are so easily fooled, for identical twins not only look alike, they also tend to talk alike, walk alike, and even think alike.

(6)   This raises the question "Does their similarity reflect their identical heredity or their identical environment?" In their early years, identical twins do share a virtually identical environment. They often occupy the same bed, eat the same food at the same time, play with the same toys, go to the same places, and interact with the same people. In addition, identical twins are united by an intimate relationship with each other. They are constant companions and enjoy a unique closeness. Some twins even seem to know what the other is thinking. It is not surprising, then, that identical twins resemble each other in behavior as well as appearance. But how much of this resemblance represents heredity and how much represents learning?

(7)   Some answers to this question have been provided by scientists who have studied identical twins who were separated from each other early in life and raised in different environments. More than 100 cases have been reported of identical twins who were separated in infancy or childhood and who were reunited many years later when one twin suddenly learned that he or she had a twin and tried to locate the lost twin. Such cases have provided scientists with an ideal way to study the relative influence of

heredity and environment in the shaping of an individual. The scientists theorize that since the heredity of identical twins is the same, any differences in twins who were reared separately must be due to environmental factors.

(8)   When psychologists hear about a pair of identical twins who were reared apart and later reunited, they invite the twins to participate in a special study. The twins are given numerous physical and psychological tests designed to determine what similarities and differences exist between the twins. Eyesight and hearing are tested, and blood pressure and heart rate are measured. Each twin is asked to complete a detailed record of illnesses and injuries. They are also given standardized intelligence tests, personality tests, and questionnaires about their fears, food preferences, school experiences, hobbies, and friends. In short, the twins are asked to tell as much as possible about themselves. Comparing the results of these tests has provided psychologists with some interesting information about the influence of heredity and environment.

(9)   In one classic case, identical twin boys were born to an unmarried fourteen-year-old girl. Soon after their birth, the boys were adopted by two different families. Nearly forty years later, one of the twins discovered adoption records that helped him locate his lost counterpart. When they were reunited, the twins were amazed by the abundance of similarities in their lives. First, they looked alike. They were six feet tall and weighed 180 pounds and 181 pounds, respectively. Both had brown eyes, dark hair, and the same facial features. But the similarities did not stop there. Both boys had been named Jim by their adoptive parents. Both had grown up with an adoptive brother named Larry. Both had pet dogs when they were young, and both had named the dog Toy. Both had married and divorced women named Linda and later married women named Betty. One had named his first son James Allan, and the other had named his first son James Alan. Both had worked at a McDonald's restaurant, and both had worked as gas station attendants. Both had taken training in law enforcement and enjoyed carpentry and drafting as hobbies. Both drove the same make of automobile, and both vacationed each year at the same beach in Florida. Also, scientists who studied the men found that they both had high blood pressure and had the same heartbeat and brainwave patterns. The men also had similar fingerprints and similar handwriting. Videotapes made of the two Jims showed that they used similar facial expressions when they talked, had similar postures when they walked, and had the same distinctive habit of pulling their hair when they read.

(10)   The lives of the two Jims abounded with similarities, but not all the pairs of reunited twins studied by the scientists had led such parallel lives. However, all the twin pairs showed a high degree of similarity in physical traits, such as height, weight, facial features, eyesight, and physique. Since these inherited physical traits persisted even though the twins were reared in different environments, scientists concluded that inherited physical traits are relatively unaffected by environmental factors.

(11)   Scientists were surprised by the high degree of similarity shown by the twins in their study in such features as voice quality, gestures, and body language. It was previously thought that children learned these traits from the people they associated with, but the twin studies led scientists to conclude that these traits are probably inherited rather than learned.

(12)   Unlike physical traits, psychological traits are not easily measured. There-fore, the twin studies did not clearly distinguish the relative effects of heredity and environment on personality. Most of the twin pairs studied showed a high degree of similarity in intelligence, interests, talents, temperaments, and life styles, but the de-gree of similarity was lower for personality traits than for physical traits. It appears that people probably inherit a tendency toward certain psychological characteristics, but that these characteristics can be influenced by environmental factors.

(13)   One particularly interesting finding in the twin studies was that identical twins who were reared apart were often more alike in personality traits than identical twins who were reared together. Psychologists account for this phenomenon by sug-gesting that twins brought up together often make a deliberate effort to be different from each other in order to establish their individuality. When reared apart, identical twins are apparently more likely to follow their natural tendencies.

(14)   Scientists caution that the twin studies are inconclusive and do not clearly distinguish between what is inherited from what is learned. Physical traits seem most influenced by heredity and least influenced by environment. In terms of personality traits, heredity seems to establish a potential for what a person can be, but environment determines what a person actually becomes. Scientists point out that so many interre-lated factors are involved in shaping an individual that it may be virtually impossible to separate the complex effects of heredity and environment.

Comprehension Check

The purpose of this activity is to check your understanding of the article and to give practice using vocabulary words. Label each sentence true or false according to the article. If you cannot understand the meaning of a sentence, use a dictionary to look up key words.

 1. Identical twins are always the same sex.
 2. Identical twins begin life from two separate ova.
 3. Fraternal twins result from a single pregnancy.
 4. Identical twins who have been reared apart tend to resemble each other physically.
 5. Identical twins who have been reared apart share a virtually identical environ-ment.
 6. Studies of identical twins who have been reared apart clearly show that personal-ity traits are inherited.
 7. Identical twins are more alike in physique than in personality.
 8. Identical twins are often indistinguishable.
 9. Heredity establishes a potential for personality traits.
10. Scientists try to reunite twins who were separated in infancy.

UNDERSTANDING WORDS

Vocabulary List

Verbs	Nouns	Adjectives/ Participles	Adverbials
conclude	abundance	identical	unlike
determine	appearance	indistinguishable	virtually
influence	behavior	physical	
inherit	characteristic	psychological	
resemble	environment	reunited	
result	feature	similar	
separate	heredity	unique	
	individual		
	personality		
	phenomenon		
	physique		
	relationship		
	role		
	sibling		
	trait		

Subject-Specific Vocabulary

Verb: rear.   **Nouns:** embryo, fertilization, gene, ovum/ova, pregnancy, sperm, twin(s).
Adjective: fraternal.   **Adverb:** genetically.

Activity 1

Use words from the previous chart to complete these sentences.

1. Identical twins are often virtually indistinguishable in _____.

2. Sometimes twins who were separated in infancy are _____ many years later.

3. Physical traits are more easily measured than _____ traits.

4. Siblings may have similar behavior traits because their parents tend to _____ them in a similar way.

5. Scientists want to find out how psychological traits are related to heredity and _____.

6. The phenomenon of fraternal twins _____ when two separate ova are fertilized.

7. Environment seems to _____ personality characteristics more than physical characteristics.

8. Eye color, hair color, and physique are physical features that are determined by

   _____.

9. Identical twins _____ each other in appearance and behavior.

10. Unlike the relationship between a child and an ordinary _____, the relationship between identical twins is very close.

11. Except for identical _____, each individual receives a unique combination of genes from his or her parents.

Activity 2

Put an **H** before each trait that is determined by heredity and an **E** before each trait that is determined by environment. Explain your answers.

hair color	height	weight	sex
nationality	race	name	religion

Activity 3

Cross out the one word that does not have the same meaning as the other three words.

1. Nowadays agencies rarely (divide/separate/unite/part) pairs of twins when they are adopted.
2. It is difficult for parents to (establish/raise/rear/bring up) twins.
3. Each (person/human/sibling/individual) has a unique personality.
4. Identical twins are (almost/nearly/virtually/really) identical physically.
5. Physical (traits/roles/characteristics/features) are inherited.
6. Scientists study the (contribution/effect/role/cause) of environment in shaping personality.
7. Our heredity is (determined/set/known/established) at the time of fertilization.
8. Personality is partially influenced by (learning/environment/potential/experience).
9. The birth of twins was considered an unnatural (event/phenomenon/relationship/occurrence) in some cultures.

Activity 4

To *influence* something refers to one of several factors that will affect the result.

> *A child's age influences the kind of books she will like. Her friends, her interests, and her intelligence might also influence her choice in books.*

To *determine* something refers to the one factor that will affect the result.

> *The size of a child's foot determines the size of shoe she will need to buy.*

Circle the word that best completes each sentence.

1. The price of a book (determines/influences) how much sales tax you will pay.
2. The size of a house (influences/determines) its price.
3. The number of chairs in a classroom (influences/determines) how many people can be seated.
4. The weather (determines/influences) how much ice cream a store will sell.

Activity 5

The following sentence patterns are frequently used to show similarities or differences between two things or people.

> Similarities: *Like eye color, hair color is inherited.*
> Differences: *Unlike eye color, hair color can be changed.*

Using the information in the reading, complete these sentences.

1. _____ ordinary siblings, fraternal twins may or may not resemble each other.

2. _____ fraternal twins, identical twins are genetically identical.

3. _____ fraternal twins, identical twins result from a single pregnancy.

4. _____ identical twins, fraternal twins are genetically related.

5. Unlike fraternal twins, identical twins develop from _____ fertilized ovum.

6. _____ ordinary siblings, identical twins share a virtually identical environment.

7. _____ identical twins reared together, identical twins reared apart tend to have the same physical characteristics.

8. By studying sets of identical twins who were separated in infancy and reared apart, scientists have concluded that _____ physical traits, personality traits seem to be inherited.

9. _____ _____ twins, _____ _____ are always the same sex.

Activity 6

Substitute a synonym from the vocabulary list for each word or group of words in parentheses. Be sure to keep the original meaning of the sentence.

1. Each (person) is (unlike any other), although (brothers and sisters) tend to (look like) each other.
2. The way children are (raised) by their parents can (affect) their (actions).
3. Identical twins are (nearly) (the same) in (the way they look).
4. (Personality) (characteristics) seem to be more easily influenced by factors in the (surroundings) than are (biological) (features).
5. If the original (egg) (divides) two times, identical triplets (occur).
6. (Microscopic bits of protein that carry genetic information) determine what we (receive) from our parents.
7. The complex (part) that heredity plays in (causing) personality (traits) is not completely clear.
8. There is an (ample quantity) of evidence proving that certain diseases are passed on (by genes).

> Unique means that nothing else like it exists. Some people make the error of saying, ''The movie was very unique. It was the most unique movie I have ever seen.'' Instead they should say, ''The movie was unique. I have never seen another one like it.''

Activity 7

Sometimes we can define an unfamiliar object by naming a familiar object that it resembles. Define the objects in the first column by telling what each resembles.

1. a coyote	a chicken
2. a zebra	a dog
3. a dolphin	a snake
4. an eel	a horse
5. a turkey	a fish

Activity 8

Which of the following pairs of items are indistinguishable?

1. a glass of Coca Cola/a glass of Pepsi Cola
2. a female chicken/a male chicken
3. a cooked egg/an uncooked egg
4. a radio that is turned on/a radio that is turned off

> Some speakers of English distinguish between the verbs to raise
> and to rear. They claim that you raise animals, but you rear
> children. Other speakers say that you can raise both animals
> and children. Everyone agrees that you can raise animals and
> vegetables, but you cannot rear vegetables.

Activity 9

The bacteria in this drawing are virtually indistinguishable. Find the one that is unique.

Activity 10

The word *virtually* can be used as a synonym for *almost* and *nearly*. The word *approximately* has the same synonyms (virtually = nearly = almost; approximately = nearly = almost), but *virtually* and *approximately* cannot be used in place of each other. *Virtually* is used to describe a condition that has not been met. *Approximately* is used to show an inexact measurement of some quantity.

Substitute *virtually* or *approximately* for the underlined words.

1. The gene for blue eyes is almost absent in black races.
2. The disease smallpox has nearly disappeared in developed countries.
3. A human pregnancy lasts almost nine months.
4. It is nearly impossible for two non-twin siblings to inherit identical genes.
5. Almost 1 of every 87 births results in twins.

> Twins means two individuals. How many individuals are there in a pair of twins? What would you call one of these individuals?

Activity 11

A word analogy shows the relationship between two pairs of words. To complete an analogy, first determine the relationship between the two words in the first pair. The most common relationships are synonyms, antonyms, and examples, but others are possible.

identical : same	(synonyms)
like : unlike	(antonyms)
zebra : animal	(example)
child : children	(plural)

The second pair of words in the analogy must have the same relationship to each other as the first pair.

identical : same   AS   characteristic : *trait*

The analogy is read like this: "Identical is to same as characteristic is to trait."

Complete the analogies below with words that may or may not be on the vocabulary list.

1. unlike : like   AS   different : _____
2. physical : physique   AS   psychological : _____
3. beginning : cause   AS   ending : _____
4. raise : vegetables   AS   rear : _____
5. mother : parent   AS   sister : _____

Activity 12

In English the most common negative prefix is *un-*, as in the word *unnatural*, meaning "not natural." Other negative prefixes occur as well, but since their occurrence is largely unpredictable, their usage needs to be learned word by word. For example, the negative prefix *ir-* occurs only before words that begin with "r," as in *irregular*, but not all words that begin with "r" use the *ir-* prefix. The word *unromantic*, for example, uses the *un-* prefix. This list of negative prefixes shows their usages.

un-	(no restrictions)	unhappy, unpredictable
in-	(no restrictions)	inactive, insensitive
im-	(before p, b, m)	impossible, immature
ir-	(before r)	irrational, irregular
il-	(before l)	illiterate, illegal

Change each phrase below to a word with a negative prefix. You may need to use a dictionary to learn the correct form.

1. not necessary	6. not dependent	11. not religious
2. not complete	7. not certain	12. not pure
3. not perfect	8. not logical	13. not loyal
4. not responsible	9. not born	14. not capable
5. not conclusive	10. not lawful	15. not willing

Activity 13

In pairs or in small groups, discuss the following:

1. What are the characteristics of a comfortable chair? a well-designed theater?

2. Name the workers you would find in a typical restaurant. What role does each worker play in the operation of the restaurant?

3. Everyone would probably enjoy having an abundance of money. What other things would you like to have an abundance of?

4. All cultures seem to have proverbs that describe human behavior or offer rules to live by. Tell the meaning of each of the following American sayings. The first one has been done for you.
   a. Birds of a feather flock together.

   People who are similar tend to associate with each other.

   b. You can't tell a book by its cover.
   c. The tree will grow as the wind blows it.
   d. You are what you eat.
   e. Like father, like son.

Activity 14

Figure 2.1 is a family chart. The relationships are to the individual labeled "A".

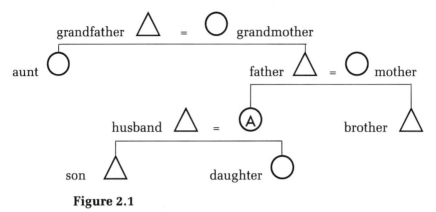

Figure 2.1

1. What symbol is used to represent a female?
2. What symbol is used to represent a male?
3. What symbol is used to represent a marriage?
4. Is individual A a male or a female?

Figure 2.2 is another family chart. Each individual has been labeled with a letter.

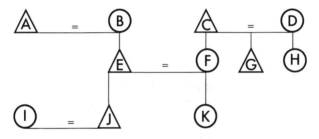

Figure 2.2

5. How many siblings does G have?
6. How many siblings does E have?
7. Which individual is not biologically related to J?
8. Which individuals are not biologically related to A?
9. What is the relationship between D and H?
10. What is the relationship between K and J?
11. What is the relationship between K and B?
12. Who is E a descendant of?

PUTTING WORDS INTO SENTENCES

Ten words have been selected from the original vocabulary list for closer study. These words and their related forms are charted below.

Verbs	Nouns	Adjectives/ Participles	Adverbials
appear	appearance	apparent	apparently
characterize	character	characteristic	characteristically
	characteristic		
	characterization		
conclude	conclusion	(in)conclusive	(in)conclusively
determine	determination	determining	
distinguish	distinction	distinct	distinctly
	distinctiveness	distinctive	distinctively
		distinguishing	
		(in)distinguishable	
individualize	individual	individual	individually
	individualization	individualized	
inherit	inheritance	inherited	
	heredity	inherent	inherently
	heritage	hereditary	
	heir		
be related (to)	relation	relative	relatively
	(inter)relationship	(inter)related	in relation (to)
	relative		
result	result	resulting	as a result (of)
unite	union	(re)united	

Activity 1

The word *distinct* means "clear" or "unmistakable." The word *distinctive* means "having a trait that allows a person to distinguish between two things."

> *The speaker's words were distinct despite the noise of the crowd.*
> *We can identify the voices of our friends on the telephone because they have distinctive voices.*

Read the paragraph below, then complete the given tasks.

To the untrained eye, all pigeons look alike, but to ornithologists and bird-watchers, the distinctiveness of each species is clearly apparent. Not only does each species have distinctive markings, but each species also makes a distinctive sound. A distinction is made between pigeons and doves on the basis of size, but there is no real difference between the two kinds of birds. In general, the larger species are referred to as pigeons and the smaller ones as doves.

Identify the birds in the diagram from their descriptions.

Red-Billed Pigeon:	uniformly dark in appearance; rounded tail
Chinese Spotted Dove:	relatively long, round tail; white marks on sides of tail; collar of black-and-white spots
Band-Tailed Pigeon:	broad, rounded tail; band of light-colored feathers on tip of tail; white strip on back of neck
Mourning Dove:	long, pointed tail; large, white spots on tail
White-Fronted Dove:	dark body with white underparts; rounded tail with white tips
White-Winged Dove:	rounded tail with white marks on tip; large white patches on wings

Activity 2

Using the characteristics above, tell how these birds can be identified. Use the words given below to form complete sentences.

1. White-Fronted Dove (distinguishable)
2. Mourning Dove (distinctive)
3. White-Winged Dove (distinct)
4. Chinese Spotted Dove (distinguish)
5. Red-Billed Pigeon (distinctively)
6. Band-Tailed Pigeon/Red-Billed Pigeon (the main distinction)

Answer these questions, using the words given.

7. How can bird-watchers identify birds by their appearance? (distinguishing)
8. How can bird-watchers distinguish between pigeons and doves? (distinguishable)

Distinguished means "noteworthy" or "having the characteristics of someone noteworthy." It is usually applicable only to humans.

> The distinguished-looking gentleman sitting over there has distinguished himself in the field of biology. His sister is a distinguished mathematician.

To have the distinction means "to be noted or honored for a unique trait or accomplishment."

> The Dionne Quintuplets had the distinction of being the first set of identical quintuplets to survive.

Activity 3

To be *related* can refer to biological connections or can show a cause-and-effect connection between events.

> *Modern reptiles are related to the extinct dinosaurs.*
> *A decrease in lung cancer is related to the crusade to encourage people to stop smoking.*

To be *interrelated* suggests that both elements in a relationship affect one another. For example:

> *The price of a product and the demand for the product are interrelated.*

In complete sentences, tell whether the following pairs of items are related or interrelated. When there is a one-way cause-effect relationship, the cause is named last.

1. athletic skill/amount of time spent practicing
2. phases of the moon/ocean tides
3. the divorce rate/the number of women working
4. the weather/the amount of wheat a farmer can grow

Activity 4

Scientists look for the relationship between one phenomenon and another. Match the names of the scientists below with the phenomena they study. Use the given word forms to make complete sentences. The first one has been done for you.

1. geneticists

   Geneticists study how birth defects are related to radiation.

2. graphologists   chimpanzees/humans (relationship)
3. anthropologists   the weather/earthquakes (interrelated)
4. phrenologists   bumps on a skull/personality (are related)
5. meteorologists   radiation/birth defects (are related)
                      handwriting/personality (is related to)

To be in a relationship or **to have a relationship**
implies a love relationship outside of marriage.
It is difficult for a divorced woman to
be in a relationship if she has children.

Activity 5

Relatively implies a comparison of one thing or event to others like it.

My neighborhood is relatively quiet. (My neighborhood is not quiet, but compared to other neighborhoods, it seems quiet.)

For each of the following lists, make a statement about the underlined item compared to the others. Use *relatively* and one of these words: low, short, few, small.

1. Height
   the average height of men in the United States   5'8"
   George Applegate   5'5"
2. Amount of sodium per 1-oz. serving of breakfast cereals

Wheatos	0 mg.	Rye Snacks	210 mg.
Oat Nuts	70	Ricies	230

3. Number of chromosomes in various species

fruit flies	2	monkeys	60
frogs	26	dogs	78
humans	46	crayfish	200

4. Diameter of planets in the Solar System

Mercury	3,100 miles	Jupiter	88,724 miles
Earth	7,926	Saturn	74,560
Mars	4,216		

A **relative** is a person related to you biologically. The term also
loosely refers to a person related to you through marriage.
You can choose your friends, but you can't choose your relatives.

Activity 6

Relative as an adjective suggests a comparison between something and others like it. For example, if you drew a diagram of the solar system that showed the *relative* sizes of the planets, Mercury would be 3″ in diameter, Earth nearly 8″ in diameter, and Jupiter more than 88″.

Rewrite these questions to include the word *relative*. The first one has been done for you.

1. How important is diet in disease prevention?

   What is the relative importance of diet in disease prevention?

2. Of what value is preschool attendance for later academic success?

3. What effect does religion have on a child's morals?

Using your own ideas or knowledge, answer the above questions using *in relation to*. For example:

Diet is very important in relation to disease prevention.

> <u>Individuality</u> refers to the uniqueness of each person. There has never been another person exactly like you, and there never will be another person exactly like you. Even identical twins are not exactly alike in every trait.

Activity 7

Read the following paragraph.

(**a**) Progressive classrooms recognize the individuality of each student. (**b**) Therefore, the teacher constantly tries to individualize the curriculum. (**c**) That is, the teacher tries to form a different course of study for each student. (**d**) An individualized program requires the teacher to give instruction to each student rather than to the class as a whole. (**e**) As a result, the students must study by themselves and must be given separate tests.

Restate the numbered sentences using the words given. You may need to add words or change the word order to make the sentences logical and grammatical.

1. (Sentence **a**) individual
2. (Sentence **b**) individualizing
3. (Sentence **c**) individualized
4. (Sentence **d**) individualization
5. (Sentence **e**) individually; individual

Activity 8

Complete the following paragraph, using word forms from the previous activity.

A good exercise program recognizes that each _____ has special needs. Therefore, the instructor tries to form an _____ exercise plan for each person. For example, _____ might mean that some people would work out on an exercise bicycle while others jogged. It takes a lot of time and expertise to _____ an exercise program, but an _____ program is best, for it meets the _____ needs of each person.

Activity 9

Read the paragraph below.

(a) In human beings the genes are contained in 23 pairs of chromosomes. (b) Sex is determined by two chromosomes, called X and Y. (c) A female's ova contain only X chromosomes, while a male's sperm contains either an X or a Y chromosome. (d) A male embryo results when a sperm containing a Y chromosome unites with a female ovum. (e) A female embryo results when a sperm containing an X chromosome unites with a female ovum.

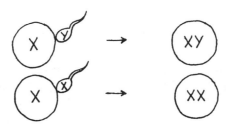

Restate the numbered sentences, using the given words.

1. (Sentence **b**) determine
2. (Sentence **b**) the determining factor
3. (Sentence **b**) the determination
4. (Sentence **d**) the union of
5. (Sentence **d**) the result is
6. (Sentence **d**) unite
7. (Sentence **e**) resulting

Activity 10

To determine has several different meanings. As used above, it means "to fix conclusively."

Genes determine the color of our eyes and hair.

To determine can also mean "to learn or find out."

Geneticists are trying to determine if certain diseases are inherited.

To be determined and *to do something with determination* mean "to have a strong or fixed purpose."

> *She worked with great determination. She was determined to finish her report before 5 o'clock.*

Tell the meaning of *determine* in each of these sentences.

1. The doctor determined from X-rays that the little girl had a heart defect.
2. The extent of the defect would determine if it could be repaired with surgery.
3. He was determined to try to save her life.
4. During surgery, he determined that the defect could be repaired.
5. The speed of her recovery would determine when she could go home.

Activity 11

As a result is used to introduce the result or conclusion after one or more statements indicating cause. Put the following statements in logical order. Add *as a result* before the result statement.

1. a. Doctors caution pregnant women over 40 that their babies may be born with Down's syndrome.
   b. The occurrence of Down's syndrome seems to be related to the age of the mother.
   c. A relatively large number of babies with Down's syndrome is born to mothers over the age of 40.
2. a. People with a perception problem known as dyslexia perceive letters and words differently from the way they are printed.
   b. Dyslexics are poor readers.
   c. Dyslexics may confuse letters like p, b, d, and q.

Activity 12

The three phrases below are used to introduce a conclusion made on the basis of observation or reasoning. The conclusion may or may not be correct, but it seems correct.

> apparently   it appears that   it is apparent that

> *Women between the ages of 35 and 39 are most likely to give birth to fraternal twins. It appears that the age of the mother is related to twin births.*

Write a conclusion for each of the following statements. Begin the conclusion with one of the above phrases.

1. Identical twins reared apart are usually more similar in height than in weight.
2. Parents often give identical twins names that sound similar, such as Jane and Joan.
3. The Yoruba people of Nigeria annually celebrate Twins Day with dancing and gift giving.

Activity 13

Newspapers must frequently print stories before all the facts are known. As a result, they often use *apparent* to indicate what the facts seem to be.

A small plane crashed during an apparent attempt to land on the beach.

Restate the short newspaper story below in four different ways, depending on which fact is the unknown. Use *apparent* or *apparently*.

A robber, in an attempt to gain entrance to the First City Bank, entered the bank through an unlocked window.

1. a robber (?)
2. an attempt to gain entrance to the bank (?)
3. entered the bank through a window (?)
4. an unlocked window (?)

Activity 14

One meaning of *appearance* is "visible features or view by others." "Looks" is a common noun synonym.

My father's appearance has changed over the years.

Another meaning is "introduction or first view."

Cities have grown noisier since the appearance of the automobile.

Explain the meaning of each of these sentences. Some may have more than one meaning.

1. The young man was embarrassed by the appearance of the soft hair on his upper lip.
2. The appearance of brain scans has revolutionized the diagnosis of brain disorders.
3. The appearance of a newborn baby often upsets its parents.
4. Jim was surprised by the appearance of his long-lost twin.
5. Its appearance suggested that the animal had been dead for several days.

Activity 15

Behavioral scientists have noted that the following characteristics are representative of women's and men's speech patterns in conversations.

Women	Men
are more skilled verbally	speak more often
express a wider range of emotions	interrupt more often
use more polite language	tend to dominate a conversation
ask more questions	are comfortable with silence

Notice the following sentence patterns.

> Verbal skill is a characteristic of women.
> Verbal skill is characteristic of women.
> Women characteristically are more skilled verbally than men.
> Verbal skill characterizes women's speech.
> Women's speech is characterized by verbal skill.

For each of the following phrases, make a statement about one of the characteristics of women's speech or of men's speech.

1. is characteristic of
2. characterizes
3. is characterized by
4. A characteristic trait of
5. characteristically

The word character has several meanings. One refers to a part in a play or movie.
   The character Juliet should be played by a young woman.

Character can also refer to personality, particularly moral qualities.
   A child's character is formed early in life.

To call someone a character suggests that the person's behavior is unusual, and often humorous.
   My Uncle Fred was a character.

Activity 16

Women are characteristically more verbal than men. They are also *inherently* more verbal than men. *Inherently* suggests a naturally occurring quality, usually biologically determined when referring to humans or animals.

> *Women characteristically use correct language, but this trait is probably learned rather than inherent.*

Use *inherently* or *characteristically* to describe these male traits.

1. are stronger
2. have deeper voices
3. use more slang in their conversations
4. marry women younger than themselves

Activity 17

Inherently and *inherent* can also be used to describe objects or events.

> *Guns are inherently dangerous.*
> *People need to be reminded of the danger inherent in keeping guns in their homes.*

Answer the following questions, using your own opinion or knowledge. Use *inherent* or *inherently.*

1. Why is gold a desirable metal for making jewelry?
2. Why do many instructors use true-false examinations?
3. Why don't most people put sugar on fruit before eating it?

Activity 18

Complete the paragraph by using *inheritance, heredity, hereditary, inherited,* or *inherit(s).* (In some cases, more than one word is possible.)

Certain diseases are _____ . They are passed along from one generation to the next through biological _____ . One such disease is hemophilia, or "bleeder's disease," which is characterized by a defect in the clotting power of blood. Hemophilia occurs when a child _____ an X chromosome that carries this defect. Usually females, who have two X chromosomes, are protected from the defective X chromosome by a healthy X chromosome. Males have one X chromosome and one Y, which cannot protect against the disease. As a result, if a male receives just one defective X chromosome, he will suffer from this _____ disease. Although scientists cannot change a person's _____ to prevent hemophilia, modern medicine allows hemophiliacs to live relatively normal lives.

An <u>heir</u> is a person who inherits (or will inherit) money or property upon the death of another person, usually an older relative.

<u>Heritage</u> can refer to a person's biological <u>inheritance</u>, but usually refers to a person's cultural inheritance.

When Tom was named the heir to his grandfather's collection of Chinese art, he decided to learn more about his Chinese heritage.

Activity 19

The following phrases refer to the use of relevant information to establish a fact or opinion.

to *conclude* (that)
to reach a/the *conclusion* (that)
to arrive at a/the *conclusion* (that)
to come to a/the *conclusion* (that)

The doctor listened to the patient describe her symptoms and concluded that she had diabetes.

To find out if fatness is determined by heredity or environment, scientists conducted a study to compare the weights of adopted individuals with the weights of their biological parents and the weights of their adoptive parents. Use the information in Table 2.1 to write a conclusion of the study. Are the results conclusive or inconclusive? That is, do the results of the study prove without a doubt that fatness is inherited?

Table 2.1	Degree of Similarity of Sons'/Daughters' Weights			
	Biological mother	Biological father	Adoptive mother	Adoptive father
son	weak	weak	none	none
daughter	strongest	strong	none	none

> To conclude/conclusion can also refer to endings.
> The professor concluded his lecture with a joke about monkeys. He always does something unusual at the conclusion of his lecture.

USING WORDS IN CONTEXT

Activity 1

Your instructor will dictate a paragraph about Siamese twins. After you have written the paragraph, work with a partner to fill in words you may have missed or to correct grammar and spelling. When you and your partner believe your paragraphs are correct, compare them to the one printed at the back of the book. Make any necessary corrections.

Activity 2

The following sentences are in scrambled order. Indicate their correct order by numbering them. When the sentences are read in the correct order, they will result in a coherent story.

_____ a. Chang and Eng, the most famous of all Siamese twins, were born in Siam in 1811.

_____ b. On the other hand, Eng was healthier and inherently more agreeable than his sibling, and he was also distinctly quieter.

_____ c. Soon the boys learned to walk and run together and had a relatively normal childhood.

_____ d. Chang had the dominant character, but he was often irritable.

_____ e. In fact, Chang and Eng never talked much to each other, apparently because they had no information to communicate.

_____ f. As young men, they moved to the United States and earned a living by appearing on stage.

_____ g. Although the boys were virtually identical in appearance, their individuality became distinct.

_____ h. The babies appeared to be normal in all ways, except that they were united at the chest by a band of flesh about 5 inches long.

_____ i. Both brothers had large families. Chang and his wife had ten children, and his counterpart Eng and his wife had eleven.

_____ j. Despite the complications inherent in their lives, the two families enjoyed a relatively peaceful relationship.

_____ k. The wives lived in individual houses, and Chang and Eng divided their time equally between the two homes.

_____ l. When they were 31 years old, Chang and Eng were united in marriage to two sisters.

_____ m. Some say that Eng died as a result of fright when he realized his brother was dead.

_____ n. The brothers died at the age of 62, first Chang and then, two hours later, Eng.

Activity 3

This diagram represents the developmental patterns for fraternal twins and identical twins. In the article about twins, find the paragraphs that explain how twins develop. Reread the paragraphs. In your own words, explain the diagram below.

The diagrams below represent the various combinations of developmental patterns for triplets (three babies) and quadruplets (four babies). Describe what takes place in each developmental pattern and explain to what degree the babies will resemble each other after birth.

Triplets

Quadruplets

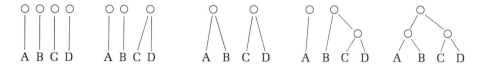

A B C D   A B C D   A B C D   A B C D   A B C D

Quintuplets

With a partner, work out the various combinations of developmental patterns for quintuplets (five babies).

Activity 4

Read the following paragraph as many times as you can in three minutes. Then with your book closed, rewrite as much of the information as you can remember.

No two individuals, not even identical twins, have identical fingerprint patterns. Because of their individuality, fingerprints are useful as a means of identification. Police often use fingerprints to determine the identity of criminals by comparing prints found at the place of a crime with the fingerprints of people who may have committed the crime. If the prints match, the police conclude that they have found the criminal. A new technique called genetic fingerprinting is now being used to identify criminals. This technique compares samples of blood or hair found at the place of a crime with samples of blood or hair taken from people who are suspected of committing the crime. Like fingerprints, elements of the genetic structure of blood and hair are individually distinctive. Recently, police in London used this technique to identify conclusively the killer of two young women.

Topics for Writing or Discussion

1. Why is the environment in which identical twins are reared more similar than the environment in which fraternal twins are reared?

2. What factors could cause identical twins to differ in appearance?

3. A child's birth order in a family is one environmental factor that can influence how the child is treated in the family. A child's sex is another factor. For example, the parents may treat the oldest child differently from the way they treat the youngest. Or they may treat sons and daughters differently. Describe some of the ways that a child's birth order and sex can influence the way he or she is reared.

4. Interest and abilities sometimes seem to run in families, perhaps as a result of both hereditary and environmental influences. Explain how both heredity and environment might produce an outstanding basketball player or a talented violinist.

The Aztec calendar stone represents the division of the solar year into eighteen months of twenty days each plus a five-day unlucky period.

3

A MEASUREMENT OF TIME

ESTABLISHING A CONTEXT

Pre-reading Discussion

- Why do people keep track of important dates on a calendar?
- Before the calendar was invented, how did people remember important dates?
- What determines the seasons?

> Read this article for general meaning. If you cannot understand the meaning of the content, use a dictionary to look up key words (words that are important to the meaning).

(1)   Every stationery store in any modern city has a large assortment of calendars and appointment books for sale. Businesses and individuals are dependent on these for daily, weekly, and monthly planning. The need to plan ahead and to keep track of appointments and daily events has made calendars important items in our work and our personal lives.

(2)   In early history, what prompted the creation of the calendar? How did humans standardize the time units of a month, a week, and a day? Using the cycles of the sun and the moon, early hunters and farmers attempted to predict rain or snow, heat or cold, and seasons for planting. Even though these early humans could predict seasons and weather cycles, they had not developed a precise way of measuring time.

(3)   The Egyptians were one of the earliest civilizations to measure time in a practical way. Accomplished in astronomy, Egyptian priests had traced the position of the stars over a period of time. They knew that every summer a particular star, Sirius, appeared on the horizon just before sunrise. The priests then came to realize that there was a relationship between the position of this star and the phenomenon of three yearly cycles of the Nile River. Once a year the river rose for a four-month period, the result of rainfall and snowmelt from near its source, and inundated its banks, adding to the richness of the soil in the surrounding area. Subsequently, crops were planted and

grown in the rich soil over a four-month period. In a final four-month cycle, the plants were harvested. In recognition of these rhythmic phases of the river—inundation, growth, and harvest—a calendar was developed to mark seasons. This calendar, one of the earliest developed, consisted of twelve months with each month having thirty days.

(4)   The Egyptian astronomers had also determined that the length of a year, based on the movement of the earth around the sun, was approximately 365 days. They had observed this cycle of a solar year as a specific time between returning seasons. To synchronize their calendar with the solar year, they added five days at the end of each year. However, they failed to account for the extra time that would accumulate over several centuries, because the actual length of a year is 365.2422 days. Thus, the Egyptian calendar progressively drifted into error over a long period of time.

(5)   Other civilizations based their calendar on phases of the moon. The ancient Babylonians developed a calendar that used lunar cycles, alternating 29- and 30-day months that roughly added up to a 354-day year. Like the Babylonians, the Greeks used a lunar cycle. In their system, two successive years had 12 lunar months and the third year had 13. The early Romans, borrowing their calendar from the Greeks, measured time from the beginning of one new moon to the next new moon, with some years having 12 new moons and others having 13. There was a problem in accounting for time in these systems because the actual movement of the moon varied over time, leading to a lack of uniformity in the dates of festivals or political events. To help overcome this confusion, the Romans had town criers who announced important dates. For example, since market dates varied from month to month, at the beginning of each month, the criers announced when market days would be held, and at the middle of the month they announced when rents were due. In effect, the town crier was a walking calendar. In fact, linguists speculate that the source of the word *calendar* may perhaps be from the Greek word *kalend*, meaning "I cry."

(6)   What seemed to be needed in these various cultures was a common way to hold people together for making plans and for determining such matters as the planting of crops and the delivery of goods. Confusion remained as to the uniform establishment of important dates.

(7)   Julius Caesar played an important role in establishing a more uniform calendar. While on a military campaign in Egypt, he learned of the Egyptian calendar, studied the system, and recognized its inaccuracies. With the help of an astronomer, Caesar designed a new calendar which was adopted in the year 47 B.C. and became known as the Julian or Roman calendar. The major differences between the Egyptian calendar and this calendar were that in the new calendar, the use of the moon to calculate time was disregarded, the number of days for each month varied, and six extra days were included by adding one day to the end of each odd-numbered month, with February having 30 days once every four years. Augustus Caesar later changed the number of days in August from 30 to 31 and deleted a day from February, establishing the present formula for leap year. This calendar was used continuously throughout the Middle Ages and as late as the 16th century.

(8)   The modern calendar now used in the Western Hemisphere, known as the Gregorian calendar, came into being in 1582 when Pope Gregory attempted to reform the calendar so that specific dates would coincide with the four seasons. He adjusted the calendar so that March 21 would always coincide with the vernal equinox, the 24-hour period in the spring when day and night are of equal length. Another adjustment was to allow for the extra day that would accumulate over several centuries, a fact that the Egyptians and Caesar had overlooked or considered to be unimportant. The pope ordered that a day would be added in century years that could be divided by 400, such as 1600 and 2000. Thus, the year 2000 will be a ''leap year,'' a year in which there are 366 days rather than 365. The Gregorian calendar basically resembled the Julian calendar, but it was more precise than any previous calendar because it coincided more accurately with the length of the solar year.

(9)   Even though the Julian and Gregorian calendars were no longer based on the lunar cycle, many Christian religious celebrations, including the celebration of Easter, continued to be tied to the cycles of the moon. Throughout history, religious groups have disagreed as to the date for Easter because of the difficulty in predicting phases of the moon very far into the future. Consequently, today Easter Sunday continues to be observed on different dates in different parts of the world.

(10)   The lunar calendar is still used in some cultures, such as the Hebrew, the Islamic, and the Chinese. These cultures mark traditional dates, such as the beginning of the new year, according to the lunar cycles; thus, the date varies. In the Chinese culture, the new year is observed somewhere between January 20 and February 20. For commerce, however, these cultures use the western, or Gregorian, calendar.

(11)   Unlike the measurement of years and months, the length of the week is not based on a cycle of nature. It was originally based on need and spontaneous agreement. The early Romans, for example, worked in the fields seven days and went into town on the eighth day to rest and participate in local festivities, thus organizing themselves with an eight-day week. This time unit was eventually changed in the third century A.D. when Emperor Constantine converted to Christianity and followed the Old Testament model of the seven-day week. The Jews followed the religious dictates of the biblical commandment to rest on the seventh day (the Sabbath), and they preserved that day for holy observances. As Christianity expanded, the seven-day week came into common use in western Europe and later in America. Ultimately, the time unit of a seven-day week was the result of both work schedules and religious practice.

(12)   In contrast to the development of the length of the week, the naming of the days of the week evolved partially from early study of the planets and partially from Roman religious beliefs. The Romans named seven planets after deities. Roman astrologers believed that each of the seven major planets influenced an hour, and through a cycle of hours and days, each planet governed the first hour of a day. Consequently, in the Romance languages (French, Spanish, and Italian, for example), the weekday names were designated according to the names of the planets. In Spanish, Monday is Lunes (Moonday), Tuesday is Martes (Mars), Wednesday is Miercoles (Mercury), Thursday is Jueves (Jupiter), Friday is Viernes (Venus), and Saturday is Sabado (Saturn). In English, on the other hand, the day names came from Norse, Gothic, and

Germanic gods and godesses. For example, Tuesday in Old English was named Tiwsday after the god Tiw, Wednesday after the god Woden, Thursday after the god Thor, Friday after the goddess Frig, and Saturday after the god Seterne. Christian missionaries added the days Sunday and Monday, the day of the sun and the day of the moon, respectively.

(13)   The concept of accounting for time on a monthly, weekly, and daily basis, resulting in the development of the calendar, partially came about through the scientific study of astronomy and the cycles of nature. But more important, it came about as the result of human need—the need to predict weather and seasons, to find a common way to make plans within communities, and to establish important dates for celebrations of historical, political, and religious significance.

Comprehension Check

The purpose of this activity is to check your understanding of the article and to give practice using vocabulary words. Label each sentence true or false according to the article. If you cannot understand the meaning of a sentence, use a dictionary to look up key words.

1. An early method of keeping track of time was prompted by the need to predict seasons, weather, and temperature.
2. An early means of establishing seasons was based on the relative position of the stars.
3. The Babylonians used the concept of the solar year as a measurement of time.
4. The Egyptian year consisted of three seasons, beginning with the annual inundation of the area around the Nile River.
5. The Greek month was based on a lunar cycle.
6. Within the early Babylonian, Greek, and Roman cultures, there was uniformity in the marking of dates.
7. Before Julius Caesar, calendar makers overlooked any inaccuracy resulting from irregularity of the lunar cycles.
8. The Julian calendar disregarded the lunar cycles to calculate the length of a month.
9. Religious groups are in agreement today as to the date for the observance of Easter Sunday.
10. The Gregorian calendar was more precise than any previous calendar.

UNDERSTANDING WORDS

Vocabulary List

Verbs	Nouns	Adjectives/ Participles	Adverbials
accumulate	concept	practical	eventually
base (on)	cycle	precise	roughly
calculate	inaccuracy	previous	subsequently
coincide	phases	rhythmic	ultimately
consist (of)	recognition	spontaneous	
disregard	significance	successive	
inundate	uniformity		
observe			
overcome			
predict			
prompt			
speculate			
synchronize			

Subject-Specific Vocabulary

Nouns: astrologer, astronomer, astronomy, deity, leap year, vernal equinox.
Adjective: lunar.

Activity 1

Substitute a synonym in the vocabulary list for each word or group of words in parentheses. Be sure to keep the original meaning of the sentence.

1. Sun dials are not (easily used) for telling time because they are not (exact).

2. The western calendar (finally) overcame (errors) caused by the changing (stages) of the moon.

3. Originally the length of a week lacked uniformity. The seven-day week was (founded on) need and (unplanned) agreement.

4. National holidays of the greatest (importance) are often in (memory) of a historical event or a great person.

5. Egyptian astronomers were responsible for the (idea) that the position of the sun and stars passed through annual (periods).

6. Comets are celestial bodies that appear in the atmosphere at regular intervals. Sometimes their appearances (happen at the same time) with a natural phenomenon, such as an earthquake, which in the past made people (theorize) that the comets were bad omens.

Activity 2

Use words from the vocabulary list to complete the following sentences:

1. Egyptian priests noticed the regularity of phases of the Nile River and its
_____ rise and fall each year.

2. One of the earliest calendars _____ 12 months of thirty days each.

3. The Egyptians added five days to the year in order to _____ their
calendar with the solar year.

4. Babylonians also measured seasons according to _____ cycles
and used a calendar of 354 days.

5. The Romans used town criers to _____ the confusion caused by a
lack of _____ in marking dates.

6. Julius Caesar recognized the _____ of the lunar calendar. This
prompted the Romans to _____ the lunar _____.

7. To allow for the extra day that would _____ over time, Pope Gregory
adjusted the _____ _____ cycle to include century years
divisible by 400.

8. The Gregorian calendar was more _____ than the Julian calendar because it _____ more accurately with the solar year.

9. There was disagreement on the date to _____ Easter because it was
difficult to _____ the _____ of the moon.

Activity 3

Cross out the one word that does not have the same meaning as the underlined word.

1. After <u>accumulating</u> a ton of waste material, industrialists must decide where to
dump it.
a. getting   b. collecting   c. growing

2. The desire for profit <u>prompts</u> auto manufacturers to change the design and features
of their models each year.
a. causes   b. inspires   c. increases

3. If you <u>disregard</u> a traffic law, such as a speed limit, you may have your driver's
license suspended.
a. respect   b. ignore   c. overlook

4. Before the invention of the automobile, <u>previous</u> societies relied on animals for
transportation.
a. prior   b. earlier   c. subsequent

5. Franklin D. Roosevelt was the only individual to serve three <u>successive</u> terms of office as U.S. president.
   a. successful   b. consecutive   c. one after the other
6. An insect passes through various <u>phases</u> of development—egg, larva, pupa, and adult.
   a. types   b. periods   c. stages
7. Scientists <u>speculate</u> that the earth is billions of years old.
   a. think   b. guess   c. decide
8. July 4 is when Americans <u>observe</u> Independence Day.
   a. celebrate   b. recognize   c. demonstrate
9. Western calendar makers <u>eventually</u> agreed on a means of observing holidays that coincided with the phases of the moon.
   a. finally   b. ultimately   c. roughly

Activity 4

Complete these analogies with words that may or may not be from the vocabulary list. The words in the second pair should have the same relationship to each other as the words in the first pair.

    Example: big : small   AS   tall : short

    1. same : identical   AS   precise :
    2. difference : sameness   AS   precision :
    3. before : after   AS   previously :
    4. easy : difficult   AS   irregular :
    5. observe : observation   AS   predict :
    6. speculate : guess   AS   conquer :

Activity 5

Put an **N** by events that are determined by a natural phenomenon, an **H** by events that were the result of human decision, and a **B** by those that may be both.

_____ phases of the moon   _____ weekday names
_____ solar cycle   _____ seasons
_____ time for harvesting crops   _____ Easter Sunday
_____ daylight savings time   _____ position of the stars
_____ sunrise and sunset   _____ the vernal equinox
_____ the length of the week   _____ the first day of the month

Activity 6

Words that refer to any person, place, thing, or idea are called common nouns. Words that refer to particular places, persons, objects, ideas, etc., are called proper nouns and are capitalized.

Common	Proper
woman	Joan of Arc
city	Paris
river	Nile River

Not all capitalized words can be found in the dictionary. Usually, only proper nouns of historical or geographical significance are included.

Skim the article and find as many proper nouns as you can and then categorize them according to the headings below.

Languages	Planets
Place Names	People
Time periods (days, months, etc.)	Deities
Nationalities or ethnic groups	Religions

Activity 7

Look up *deities* in your dictionary. What base word do you find?

_____

How does the spelling of the word change when it is pluralized?

_____

Use the verb form in the following sentence:

King Louis XIV of France was _____ and was called the Sun King.

Many words such as *deity* undergo a spelling change when pluralized or when used in the past tense or as modifiers. What is the base word of each of the following words?

Derived form	Base word	Derived form	Base word
predicting	predict	precision	
coincidental		overcame	
uniformity		rhythmically	
observance		inaccuracies	

Activity 8

To determine the meaning of *vernal equinox*, look up *vernal* in the dictionary.

What is the meaning of the base *equi*? _____

Explain the meaning of *vernal equinox* in your own words.

What is the *autumnal equinox*, and what is its date? _____

Match the words on the left with the drawings. Explain the meaning of *equa* or *equi* in these words.

1. equator
2. equation
3. equivalent
4. equidistant

$$2 + 2 = 4$$

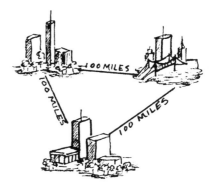

1 kilogram and 2.2 pounds

February has 28 days, and every four years it has 29. In the 20th century, there are 24 leap year days. In a century year that can be divided evenly by 400, an extra day is added. So in the years 2000, 2400, and 2800, February will have 29 days, and there will be 366 days in those years.

Activity 9

Familiar expressions are often used to give practical advice. Match these expressions with their meanings.

Look before you leap.	Don't disregard small problems. They often reflect larger problems.
Where there is smoke, there is fire.	Don't make spontaneous decisions. Observe the circumstances before you do something.
Don't leap to conclusions.	Don't base your ideas on information that may have no significance. Wait until you accumulate accurate information.

Activity 10

In the article, reference is made to *astrology* and *astronomy*. *Astrology* is the art of understanding the supposed influence of the heavenly bodies (stars and planets) on human affairs. *Astronomy* is the scientific study of the sun, moon, stars, and other heavenly bodies. To distinguish between these two concepts, categorize the following statements under either *astronomy* or *astrology*.

1. You will inherit a fortune soon.
2. The explosion of a supernova was observed through the telescope.
3. Aquarius coincides with Scorpio this month—a bad omen.
4. The distance between the earth and its sun is 92,900,000 miles.
5. The Gemini twins is one of twelve astrological signs that are influenced by the planets.
6. You will be reunited with a long-lost relative.
7. Mars has a red glow caused by areas of iron oxide.
8. The measurement of the speed of a star as it moves through space toward or away from a planet is called radial velocity.

Activity 11

Three words used in the article on calendars are related to the concept of time: *eventually*, *subsequently*, and *ultimately*. *Subsequently* means "following in time or order": one action follows another action, and the actions have a relationship. *Subsequently* is sometimes confused with *consequently*, which means "as a result" or "therefore." Consider these examples:

> *Julius Caesar learned about the Egyptian calendar while on a military crusade. Subsequently, he consulted an astronomer and made changes in the Roman calendar.*

> *Caesar recognized the superior features of the Egyptian calendar and, consequently, made changes in the Roman calendar.*

Ultimately means "finally" or "being at the end."

> *After test-driving several cars, Henry ultimately decided on a Mercedes.*

Eventually means something happening after a relatively long period of time.

> *Scientists speculate that the sun will eventually burn itself out.*

Eventually and *ultimately* have similar meanings, but the focus is different in terms of time. *Eventually* focuses on the length of time for something to be accomplished, whereas *ultimately* focuses on the completion of an action. Explain the difference in the pairs of sentences below.

a. Eventually everyone dies.
b. Ultimately everyone dies.

a. If you drink too much, you will eventually get drunk.
b. If you drink too much, you will ultimately get drunk.

a. When exposed to water, iron will eventually rust.
b. When exposed to water, iron will ultimately rust.

Activity 12

The pictures below show successive events. Explain what happened first, subsequently, ultimately, and consequently.

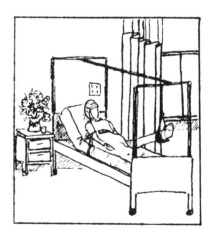

Activity 13

List successive phases of the following cycle:

human life: fertilization, _____, birth, infancy, _____,

_____, _____, death.

Activity 14

To *accumulate* means "to make or become greater in quantity." It suggests an excessive amount over a period of time. What accumulates can be something material, such as trash, or it can be abstract, such as an amount of work to be done.

Trash began to accumulate in the vacant lot.
While I was on vacation, the work at my office accumulated.

Which of the following are easy to accumulate?

debts	traffic tickets	souvenirs	silver dollars
college degrees	aluminum cans	junk mail	pennies

Activity 15

In pairs or in small groups, discuss the following questions:

1. Which of these activities do you consider rhythmic?

singing	swimming	dancing	sleeping
thinking	typing	breathing	speaking

2. In what occupations do people make predictions?

3. What could happen if you were to disregard the following?

a law	directions on a prescription
a warning	a ringing telephone
a doctor's order	a traffic signal
directions in a recipe	someone flirting with you

4. Which of the following are usually spontaneous?

laughter	breakfast	arguments
investments	marriage	vacations

5. What do you do when you are inundated with homework assignments? What else could you be inundated with?

6. In the following pairs, which is more practical?
   a. buying a blouse or flowers
   b. taking a trip by car or by train
   c. buying generic brand products or name-brand products
   d. communicating in your mother tongue or a second language

7. What could happen if the clocks in hospitals or airports were not synchronized?

8. What is the historical significance of each of these events?
   a. World War I
   b. launch of the first manned spacecraft
   c. discovery of America
   d. discovery of oil
   e. invention of the automobile
   f. development of a microcomputer
   g. invention of television
   h. World War II
   i. development of nuclear energy

9. What prompted each of the above events?

10. Which of the following has an inaccuracy?

    325 × 3 = 975   1043 − 15 = 1018   3478 + 589 = 4067

11. In which of the sentences below could you substitute the word *roughly*?
    a. The basketball captain is almost 7 feet tall.
    b. It's practically 6:00. It's 5:58.
    c. The library usually closes at 10:00. On Friday it closes at 9:00.
    d. The mountain climbers hardly made it to the top of the mountain because they ran out of supplies.
    e. The company president retired after 30 years and eleven months. He worked for about 31 years.

12. What do the following consist of?

a minute	a month	a week	a decade
an hour	a year	a month	a century
a day	a leap year		

PUTTING WORDS INTO SENTENCES

Ten words have been selected from the original vocabulary list for closer study. These words and their related forms are listed below.

Verbs	Nouns	Adjectives/ Participles	Adverbials
accumulate	accumulation	accumulative cumulative	
base (on)	basis	basic	basically
calculate	calculation calculator	calculating	
coincide	coincidence	coincidental	coincidentally
disregard	disregard	disregarded	
regard	regard		regardless (of)
inundate	inundation	inundated	
observe	observance observation	observant observable	
predict	prediction	(un)predictable	predictably
recognize	recognition	(un)recognizable recognized	recognizably
speculate	speculation speculator	speculative	

Activity 1

An *accumulation* of something means that a great quantity has piled up or built up over time. *To accumulate* can be transitive or intransitive. The subject of the intransitive form in most cases is non-human.

> *People accumulate pennies.*
> *Pennies accumulate quickly.*

Accumulative has an alternate form, *cumulative*.

> *The student's cumulative (accumulative) grade point average was 3.5.*

Reword the sentences below, using the word form in parentheses. You may have to add or delete words, and/or change the word order.

1. Because of construction next door, there was a buildup of dust. (accumulated)
2. After the storm, trash had gathered on the beach. (accumulation of)
3. After years of piling up debts, the bank was forced to close down. (cumulative effect)
4. After many trips to Europe, I had collected many souvenirs. (accumulation of)
5. By the age of ten, a child has built up a great deal of information. (accumulates)

Activity 2

To base a calendar *on* the seasons means to use the seasons as a foundation for the calendar. Notice that when the active form of the verb is used, the two words of the verb form are separated by the object of the verb.

> *Scientists **base** their theories **on** investigation and experimentation.*

The passive form is not separated.

> *Their theories are based on investigation and experimentation.*

Basis refers to the elements from which something is created, developed, or calculated. It usually refers to something abstract.

> *The basis of the lunar calendar is cycles of the moon.*

Basic means that something is more necessary than anything else, or it is what everything else depends on.

> *The basic ingredients of bread are flour, yeast, and water.*
> *Proper diet is basic to good health.*

Basically has to do with what is most important. It means "in reality" or "fundamentally."

> *Even though Jim cheats at cards, he is basically an honest person.*

Using *basic, basis, based on,* and *basically,* write sentences combining the information below.

1. Darwin's theory of evolution   man evolved from apes
2. study habits   success in college
3. star   a mass of gas
4. western calendar   solar cycle
5. lunar cycle   Muslim calendar

Activity 3

One meaning of *to calculate* is applied to the idea of mathematical computation. It means "to figure or estimate."

> *The truck driver calculated that the trip would take five hours at 55 miles per hour.*

Restate the numbered sentences, using the word forms in parentheses. You may need to add words or change the word order to make the sentences logical.

1. Scientists have computed that there are at least 100 million, million, million stars in the universe. (scientific calculation)
2. Using statistical data, astronomers figure that the outer edge of the universe is about 10 million light years from earth. (basing . . . calculate)
3. Founding their theory on scientific study, astronomers estimate that a galaxy may contain from 10 thousand to a million stars. (base . . . calculate)

A <u>calculating</u> person is one who is shrewd or manipulative.
The calculating businesswoman bought all of the land
surrounding her property.
It was a calculated move to expand her investments.

Activity 4

To predict something or *to make a prediction* of something always refers to future time.

> *The weatherman predicted that it would rain before Wednesday.*
> *Meteorologists make weather predictions on the basis of atmospheric changes.*

To predict is often followed by "that" or by question words such as "how," "when," and "what."

> *No one can accurately predict what the future holds.*
> *Lacking adequate information, seismologists can't predict when an earthquake will strike.*

Predictable and *predictably* refer to actions that are expected or are easy to predict.

> *The monsoon season in India is predictable.*
> *The fields are predictably flooded every year.*

Write sentences using the word groups below. You may have to change the word order or add words to make grammatical and logical sentences.

1. prediction/fortune teller/future/based
2. predict/prophet/when
3. predictable/calculations/outcome
4. the prediction/astrologer/star signs
5. predictably/fell apart/inferior product
6. predict/what/10 years/your life

Activity 5

To disregard something means ''to ignore'' something.

To have a disregard for something means ''to lack respect or concern for'' something.

> *She had a disregard for doctors, so she disregarded her doctor's advice to quit smoking.*

To regard means ''to consider'' and is often used with phrases beginning with ''as.''

> *Americans regard time as a commodity that can be spent, saved, or wasted.*

To highly regard something or *to have a high regard for* something means ''to respect'' it.

> *I highly regard my chemistry professor.*
> *I have a high regard for my chemistry professor.*
> *I have the highest regard for my chemistry professor.*

Regardless of means ''without concern for'' or ''despite.''

> *Mary continued smoking regardless of the doctor's advice.*

Read the following paragraph.

(a) In the 15th century, uneducated people still thought that the world was flat. (b) However, scientific theory toward the end of the century led some people to believe that the world was round. (c) Ignoring popular belief, Christopher Columbus sailed off to find India and to bring riches back to Spain. (d) In spite of the danger, Columbus believed his mission was important. (e) Without concern for the risk involved, Columbus and his crew sailed onward and eventually discovered the New World.

Restate the numbered sentences, using the words given. You may need to add words or change word orders to make the sentences logical and grammatical.

1. (Sentence **a**) regarded
2. (Sentence **b**) regard
3. (Sentence **c**) disregarded
4. (Sentence **d**) regardless
5. (Sentence **e**) disregarding

> Regards as a plural noun means "good wishes."
> After giving his regards to Queen Isabella, Columbus described the wonders of his voyage.

Activity 6

To inundate and *inundation* are usually associated with the flooding of water, such as after a heavy rain. This is the literal meaning of the word. A figurative meaning is associated with excess, or a feeling of being overwhelmed by something.

> *People inundated the police department with phone calls after the earthquake. (A flood of phone calls came in to the police department.)*

Imagine that you are a news reporter and you are reporting the news of a flood. Complete the sentences below, using *inundate, inundated,* and *inundation.*

1. The river rose to the top of the river bank, and _____

   _____.

2. The river overflowed; subsequently, _____

   _____.

3. The people living near the river fear that _____

   _____.

4. So many people were left homeless that the Red Cross _____

   _____.

Activity 7

One meaning of *to observe* is "to act in accordance with laws and customs." The customs might include holidays and celebrations of special events. When this meaning is intended, the noun form is *observance.*

> *Easter is observed on different dates in different cultures.*
> *The observance of Easter is of religious importance to Christians.*

Use the word forms in parentheses to answer the following questions.

1. Name a religious holiday that is celebrated in a culture that you are familiar with. (observe)
2. On what date is Christmas celebrated in the western world? (observance)
3. What two American presidents are honored on their birthdays in February? (observed)
4. What day in July is set aside by Americans to celebrate the signing of the Declaration of Independence? (in observance of)

> Another meaning of <u>to observe</u> is "to see and notice." When this meaning is intended, the noun form is <u>observation</u>. The adjective form <u>observant</u> refers to someone who is quick or especially skillful at noticing something.
>
> Leonardo DaVinci was very observant.
> While relaxing in a park, he observed the flight of birds.
> His observation led him to design an airplane with flapping wings.

Activity 8

To speculate means "to reflect or think about something that may or may not be true." It may refer to the past, present or future. When referring to the future, to speculate has the same meaning as to predict. Notice that this verb is intransitive and is followed by a clause beginning with "that." Speculation is the noun form and speculative is the adjective form.

> Scientists speculate that skin cancer will increase as a result of the wearing away of a protective layer of gases in the atmosphere.
> Anthropologists speculate that Stonehenge was used as an ancient observatory.
> These ideas are based on speculation. They are speculative.

What might each of the following scientists predict would happen if the sun were to disppear for six months? Use to speculate or speculation in your answers.

    a. a botanist   c. a psychologist
    b. a sociologist   d. a meteorologist

Activity 9

To speculate is commonly used in the business world. In this context it means "to buy or deal in goods where a large profit might be made at considerable risk." Speculative means "risky."

> She hoped to get rich by speculating in the stock market.
> His business investments were speculative.

Refer to the information in the following paragraph to answer the questions, using the words in parentheses in your answers.

Gold is an especially speculative investment because its value is influenced by many different factors. The value of gold can increase suddenly as a result of war, economic instability, or environmental disaster. Likewise, the value of gold decreases during times of global peace and financial stability.

a. Was speculation in the gold market profitable in 1939? (speculative)

b. Was it profitable to invest in gold last year? (speculation)

c. Imagine that you had a personal friend in the Pentagon, and that you received privileged information that a world war would erupt in two days. Would you invest in gold? (would speculate)

d. Why are people cautious about investing in gold? (speculating)

Activity 10

When two events occur at the same time, they are *coincidental* or they happen *coincidentally*. One event *coincides* with the other, and together they form a *coincidence*.

> *Thunder occurs coincidentally with lightning.*

The noun *coincidence* emphasizes the element of chance of two unrelated events occurring at the same time.

> *John Adams, the second U.S. president, died on July 4, 1826. By coincidence, Thomas Jefferson, the third president, died on the same day. It was a coincidence that this day was also the observance of the 50th anniversary of the Declaration of Independence.*

Restate each of the sentences below, using the given word.

1. In some years, the Jewish festival Passover is at the same time as the Christian holiday Easter. (coincidentally)
2. The three-day Vietnamese New Year festival, Tet, begins with the appearance of a new moon. (coincidental)
3. The years 1990, 1991, and 1992 match the years of the horse, the sheep, and the monkey, respectively, on the Chinese lunar calendar. (coincide).
4. The International Date Line roughly follows the 180th meridian. (coincide)
5. All five of the children of Mrs. Irma Boggs were born on April 17, but in different years. (coincidence)

Activity 11

To recognize something has several meanings: (a) to know and remember someone or something; (b) to accept something as lawful or real; (c) to see something clearly in your mind; (d) to acknowledge, or to show official gratitude for something or someone.

When the noun form *recognition* is used, it is often accompanied by the verbs "to give" or "to receive."

> *The president gave recognition to the Olympic athletes for their athletic accomplishments.*
> *The athletes received recognition from the president for their athletic accomplishments.*

Which meaning applies to this sentence from the article? "In recognition of these rhythmic phases of the river—inundation, growth, and harvest—a calendar was developed to mark seasons." _____

Which meaning applies to each of these sentences?

_____ 1. The United States recently recognized the government of the Republic of China.

_____ 2. I recognized that the employee was very capable, so I gave her a promotion.

_____ 3. The police department recognized the officer for bravery.

_____ 4. I almost didn't recognize him because he was wearing a hat and sunglasses.

_____ 5. The teenager was recognized for saving the child from drowning.

Restate the five sentences above, using the word forms as indicated.

1. recognition
2. In recognition of
3. was recognized
4. unrecognizable
5. recognition

Activity 12

The comparative form of an adjective is formed by adding -er to the adjective if the word has one syllable or if it ends in y.

> Plastic is **stronger** and **heavier** than paper.

If the word has two or more syllables, then the construction more (adjective) than or as (adjective) as is usually used.

> The Gregorian calendar was **more precise than** the Julian calendar.
> Apple computers are **as popular as** IBM computers.

The superlative adjective form uses an -est ending or the most with adjectives of more than one syllable.

> Allyson is the **smartest** child in the world.
> The western calendar is **the most accurate** calendar of any calendar that has been developed to this day.

(See glossary for further explanation.)

Choose two words from each word group and write one comparative sentence. Then use the third word to write a superlative sentence. Use precise or accurate in each sentence.

a. calculator/the human mind/ abacus
b. sun dial/hour glass/clock
c. gun/sling shot/bow and arrow
d. Julian calendar/Gregorian calendar/Egyptian calendar

USING WORDS IN CONTEXT

Activity 1

Your instructor will dictate a paragraph about the length of the day and year. After you have written the paragraph, work with a partner to fill in words you may have missed or to correct grammar and spelling. When you and your partner believe your paragraphs are correct, compare them to the one printed at the back of the book. Make any necessary corrections.

Activity 2

The following sentences are in scrambled order. Indicate their correct order by numbering them. When the sentences are in correct order, they will result in a coherent paragraph.

_____ a. A later phase was when the Babylonians developed a lunar cycle that had a year of roughly 354 days.

_____ b. Ultimately, with the changes made over centuries, the calendar has helped people to organize their daily schedules and routines in a practical way.

_____ c. Man's need to measure time prompted the development of a calendar.

_____ d. Like the Babylonians, the Greeks and Romans used a lunar cycle.

_____ e. An early phase of development can be traced to the concept of seasons based on the rhythmic phases of the Nile River.

_____ f. To deal with this problem, the Romans developed a calendar based on the solar cycle, which helped overcome the irregularities of the lunar cycle.

_____ g. This device went through several phases of development.

_____ h. The calendar is a device that measures time in cycles of days, weeks, and months.

_____ i. There was a problem with these systems based on the lunar cycle because the cycles varied from month to month.

_____ j. Other Roman developments eventually resulted in what is now called the Gregorian or western calendar.

Activity 3

Read the paragraph below as many times as you can in three minutes. Then with your books closed, rewrite as much of the information as you can remember.

In 1752, a calendar reform was adopted in America to make the calendar more accurate. One change was made that eliminated 11 days from the year, making the year shorter. Also, New Year's Day was changed from March 24 to January 1 to make the

American calendar uniform with the calendar of western Europe. These changes affected people in various ways, but a significant effect was a change in the date for the birthday celebration of President Washington, which is now observed on February 22 instead of on his actual birthday of February 11.

Activity 4

Complete the paragraph below with words from the vocabulary list.

We can predict that a child will go through specific stages of development. The basis for this _____ is the knowledge we have of the human body and its _____ of development. In the early _____, it is possible to _____ changes in a child's physical characteristics, but in later years the changes are not as observable. On the _____ of scientific observation, it is possible to accurately _____ at what age a child may begin walking or talking. However, because of individual differences, such predictions can be _____. Overall, there is a similar pattern in the development of all children even though each child becomes a unique individual.

Topics for Writing or Discussion

1. List important holidays that are observed in various countries around the world. Classify them by regions, by seasons, by calendar dates, by lunar cycles, or by any other categories you can think of. Write a short essay in which you discuss these holidays. Organize the essay according to three or four categories. Attempt to use forms of the following words: *observe, base on, recognition,* and *significant.*

2. Holidays are often observed in various countries to honor a famous person, for example, George Washington, Abraham Lincoln, or Martin Luther King, Jr. Usually these people are recognized for their deeds or achievements after their death. Write a paragraph in which you propose to establish a new holiday in recognition of someone still living who has contributed to humanity. Tell what the person has achieved and why you think there should be a special observance for this person.

3. Describe a time when you forgot an important date. What was the occasion? Why did you forget it? What ultimately happened when you learned that you forgot the date?

4. People keep track of time and organize their daily lives in different ways. How would you manage your time without the use of a calendar? What other methods or devices could you use to keep track of dates and appointments? Would these methods or devices be more or less accurate or practical than the use of a calendar?

4

PERSONAL COMPUTERS: THE EARLY YEARS

ESTABLISHING A CONTEXT

Pre-reading Discussion

- Who uses computers today? Give examples of the impact they have on our lives.
- When did the first personal computer appear? How was it different from the computers that preceded it?
- How have computers changed since the first one was introduced in the early 1940s?
- Where is the Silicon Valley? How is it related to the computer industry?

> Read this article for general meaning. If you cannot understand the meaning of the content, use a dictionary to look up key words (words that are important to the meaning).

(1)   Until the late 1970s, the computer was viewed as a massive machine that was useful to big business and big government but not to the general public. Computers were too cumbersome and expensive for private use, and most people were intimidated by them. As technology advanced, this was changed by a distinctive group of engineers and entrepreneurs who rushed to improve the designs of then-current technology and to find ways to make the computer attractive to more people. Although these innovators of computer technology were very different from each other, they had a common enthusiasm for technical innovation and the capacity to foresee the potential of computers. This was a very competitive and stressful time, and the only people who succeeded were the ones who were able to combine extraordinary engineering expertise with progressive business skills and an ability to foresee the needs of the future.

(2)   Much of this activity was centered in the Silicon Valley in northern California, where the first computer-related company had located in 1955. That company attracted

A digital signal processor chip from Bell Laboratories. This microprocessor chip supplies enough power to run a sophisticated computer system. Courtesy A.T. & T. Co. Photo/Graphics Center.

thousands of related businesses, and the area became known as the technological capital of the world. Between 1981 and 1986, more than 1000 new technology-oriented businesses started there. At the busiest times, five or more new companies started in a single week. The Silicon Valley attracted many risk-takers and gave them an opportunity to thrive in an atmosphere where creativity was expected and rewarded.

(3)   Robert Noyce was a risk-taker who was successful both as an engineer and as an entrepreneur. The son of an Iowa minister, he was informal, genuine, and methodical. Even when he was running one of the most successful businesses in the Silicon Valley, he dressed informally and his office was an open cubicle that looked like everyone else's. A graduate of the Massachusetts Institute of Technology (MIT), he started working for one of the first computer-related businesses in 1955. While working with these pioneers of computer engineering, he learned many things about computers and business management.

(4)   As an engineer, he co-invented the integrated circuit, which was the basis for later computer design. This integrated circuit was less than an eighth of an inch square but had the same power as a transistor unit that was over 15 inches square or a vacuum tube unit that was 6.5 feet square. As a businessman, Noyce co-founded Intel, one of the most successful companies in the Silicon Valley and the first company to introduce the microprocessor. The microprocessor chip became the heart of the computer, making it possible for a large computer system that once filled an entire room to be contained on a small chip that could be held in one's hand. The directors of Intel could not have anticipated the effects that the microprocessor would have on the world. It made possible the invention of the personal computer and eventually led to the birth of thousands of new businesses. Noyce's contributions to the development of the integrated circuit and the microprocessor earned him both wealth and fame before his death in 1990. In fact, many people consider his role to be one of the most significant in the Silicon Valley story.

(5)   The two men who first introduced the personal computer (PC) to the marketplace had backgrounds unlike Robert Noyce's. They had neither prestigious university educations nor experience in big business. Twenty-year-old Steven Jobs and twenty-four-year-old Stephen Wozniak were college drop-outs who had collaborated on their first project as computer hobbiests in a local computer club. Built in the garage of Jobs's parents, this first personal computer utilized the technology of Noyce's integrated circuit. It was typewriter-sized, as powerful as a much larger computer, and inexpensive to build. To Wozniak the new machine was a gadget to share with other members of their computer club. To Jobs, however, it was a product with great marketing potential for homes and small businesses. To raise the $1300 needed to fill their first orders, Jobs sold his Volkswagen bus and Wozniak sold his scientific calculator. Wozniak built and delivered the first order of 100 computers in ten days. Lacking funds, he was forced to use the least expensive materials, the fewest chips, and the most creative arrangement of components. Jobs and Wozniak soon had more orders than they could fill with their makeshift production line.

(6)   Jobs and Wozniak brought different abilities to their venture: Wozniak was the technological wizard, and Jobs was the entrepreneur. Wozniak designed the first

model, and Jobs devised its applications and attracted interest from investors and buyers. Wozniak once admitted that without Jobs he would never have considered selling the computer or known how to do it. "Steve didn't do one circuit, design or piece of code. He's not really been into computers, and to this day he has never gone through a computer manual. But it never crossed my mind to sell computers. It was Steve who said, 'Let's hold them up and sell a few.' "

(7)   From the very beginning, Apple Computer had been sensitive to the needs of a general public that is intimidated by high technology. Jobs insisted that the computers be light, trim, and made in muted colors. He also insisted that the language used with the computers be "user-friendly" and that the operation be simple enough for the average person to learn in a few minutes. These features helped convince a skeptical public that the computer was practical for the home and small business. Jobs also introduced the idea of donating Apple Computers to thousands of California schools, thereby indirectly introducing his product into the homes of millions of students. Their second model, the Apple II, was the state-of-the-art PC in home and small business computers from 1977 to 1982. By 1983 the total company sales were almost $600 million, and it controlled 23 percent of the worldwide market in personal computers.

(8)   As the computer industry began to reach into homes and small businesses around the world, the need for many new products for the personal computer began to emerge. Martin Alpert, the founder of Tecmar, Inc., was one of the first people to foresee this need. When IBM released its first personal computer in 1981, Alpert bought the first two models. He took them apart and worked twenty-four hours a day to find out how other products could be attached to them. After two weeks, he emerged with the first computer peripherals for the IBM PC, and he later became one of the most successful creators of personal computer peripherals. For example, he designed memory extenders that enabled the computer to store more information, and insertable boards that allowed people to use different keyboards while sharing the same printer. After 1981, Tecmar produced an average of one new product per week.

(9)   Alpert had neither the technical training of Noyce nor the computer clubs of Jobs and Wozniak to encourage his interest in computer engineering. His parents were German refugees who worked in a factory and a bakery to pay for his college education. They insisted that he study medicine even though his interest was in electronics. Throughout medical school he studied electronics passionately but privately. He became a doctor, but practiced only part time while pursuing his preferred interest in electronics. His first electronics products were medical instruments that he built in his living room. His wife recognized the potential of his projects before he did, and enrolled in a graduate program in business management so she could run his electronics business successfully. Their annual sales reached $1 million, and they had 15 engineers working in their living room before they moved to a larger building in 1981. It wasn't until 1983 that Alpert stopped practicing medicine and gave his full attention to Tecmar. By 1984 Tecmar was valued at $150 million.

(10)   Computer technology has opened a variety of opportunities for people who are creative risk-takers. Those who have been successful have been alert technologically, creatively, and financially. They have known when to use the help of other people and when to work alone. Whereas some have been immediately successful, others have gone unrewarded for their creative and financial investments; some failure is inevitable in an environment as competitive as the Silicon Valley. Rarely in history have so many people been so motivated to create. Many of them have been rewarded greatly with fame and fortune, and the world has benefited greatly from this frenzy of innovation.

Comprehension Check

The purpose of this activity is to check your understanding of the article and to give practice using vocabulary words. Label each sentence true or false according to the article. If you cannot understand the meaning of a sentence, use a dictionary to look up key words.

1. Robert Noyce graduated from a prestigious university and gained engineering expertise before he devised the integrated circuit.
2. Robert Noyce was one of the pioneers of the computer industry.
3. The microprocessor influenced the world in ways that its inventors did not foresee and subsequently led to the invention of the integrated circuit.
4. Stephen Wozniak and Steven Jobs used the state-of-the-art technology developed by Robert Noyce when they devised the first personal computer.
5. When Wozniak designed the first model of the PC, he did not plan to market it to the general population.
6. Jobs did not want the PC to be as intimidating to the general public as previous computers were, so he insisted that it include features that were practical and attractive.
7. The Apple Computer company sold their computers to thousands of American schools at discounted rates, thereby introducing their product into the homes of millions of students.
8. Martin Alpert foresaw that the success of the first IBM personal computer was inevitable, so he bought the first two models and devised ways to change them.
9. Martin Alpert's wife was skeptical about the potential of her husband's technical innovations.
10. Alpert's interest in technology was more passionate than his interest in medicine.

UNDERSTANDING WORDS

Vocabulary List

Verbs	Nouns	Adjectives/Participles	Adverbials
anticipate	application	cumbersome	passionately
collaborate	capacity	genuine	technologically
devise	components	inevitable	thereby
donate	entrepreneur	makeshift	whereas
emerge	expertise	massive	
foresee	gadget	muted	
intimidate	innovation	skeptical	
market	investment	state-of-the-art	
thrive	potential		
	technology		
	venture		
	wizard		
	pioneer		

Subject-Specific Vocabulary

Nouns: integrated circuit, microprocessor, circuit, peripherals.
Adjective: user-friendly.

Activity 1

Subsitute a synonym from the vocabulary list for each word or group of words in parentheses. Be sure to keep the original meaning of the sentence.

1. Steven Jobs and Stephen Wozniak (worked together) to (invent) the personal computer, and then produced it in a (temporary) production line in a garage.

2. Steven Jobs wanted to (advertise and sell) the personal computer to people who would use it in their homes, so he knew it could be neither (very large) nor (awkward).

3. Stephen Wozniak applied the (most up-to-date) (applied science) when designing the first personal computer, while Steven Jobs designed its (practical functions).

4. People seemed to be less (frightened) by computers when they were made in (soft) colors and were (easily understood by the average person).

5. Robert Noyce's (specialization) in computers was a result of his experience with the (first people) in the computer field while working at his first job.

6. Martin Alpert's wife was never (doubtful) about (the future possibilities) of Tecmar.

7. Martin Alpert studied the first IBM personal computer (with great love and emotion), and (by that means) he was the first innovator to (come forward) with (supplementary devices) for the computer.

8. Whereas some people (grow) as a result of competition, others are (threatened) by it.

Activity 2

The early computers were massive, cumbersome and intimidating. Circle the words that describe these computers.

small	awkward	inexpensive
compact	easy to understand	makeshift
enormous	concise	trim
convenient		

Activity 3

Before 1970 the general population was intimidated by computers. As a result, which of the following were true?

a. Computers seemed threatening.
b. Computers seemed exciting.
c. Computers dominated their lives.
d. Many people were frightened of computers.
e. Many people were comfortable with computers.
f. Many people were passionately interested in computers.

Activity 4

Some of the following statements describe an act of an entrepreneur (**E**), others describe an act of an inventor (**I**), and others could describe both titles (**B**). Identify each one and be prepared to explain your answer.

1. Alexander Graham Bell originated the first telephone.
2. Robert Noyce co-invented the integrated circuit and co-founded Intel.
3. In 1890 John Loud created the first ball-point pen.
4. Robert Noyce's engineering expertise contributed to the development of the microprocessor.
5. Robert Noyce's financial investments helped build one of the most successful companies in the Silicon Valley.
6. Steven Jobs had the original idea to market the first personal computer.
7. King C. Gillette designed the first disposable razor blade.
8. A Frenchman named Benedictus introduced the idea of making safety glass in 1903 after he discovered a chemical that held broken glass together.
9. Martin Alpert devised many new products for the personal computer.
10. Martin Alpert's wife managed his business and marketed his products.

Activity 5

Whereas has two meanings. The meaning must be determined by the context. One meaning is "since" or "in view of the fact that."

> *Whereas the couple had many children, they needed a large house.*

Whereas can also mean "while" or "although." When used in this way, *whereas* can be used in front of either the first or the second clause.

> *Whereas my teacher was too strict, my sister's teacher was too friendly.*
> *I like to eat vegetarian meals, whereas my husband prefers to eat beef.*

Complete the following sentences:

1. Whereas my English class focuses on vocabulary, _____
2. People in the United States speak English, whereas _____

Activity 6

Thereby means "by that means" or "connected with that reference." It always follows an independent clause (see Glossary). The verb form that follows *thereby* is always in the -ing form and refers to the subject of the first clause. Notice the following sentence patterns.

> *The Univac I could be made for $500 in 1980, thereby making it affordable for small business.*
> *He looked away from the road while he was driving, thereby causing an accident.*
> *I bought a dress, thereby spending all of my money.*

Combine the information in the following two columns. Then create sentences, connecting the information with *thereby*. For example:

> *I learned to use a computer, thereby making my life more efficient.*

1. I bought a house	improving my health
2. I studied French	satisfying my lifelong dream
3. I began exercising every day	preparing myself for my vacation
4. I learned to use a computer	making my life more efficient

Activity 7

By breaking the word *collaborate* into its parts (col labor ate), you can guess its meaning if you know that *co/col* means "with."

The first two columns contain names of people, and the third column contains names of their accomplishments. Combine the information in these columns to form sentences. Use the word "collaborated" in your answer.

Steven Jobs	Arthur Sullivan	*H.M.S. Pinafore*
Wilbur Wright	Stephen Wozniak	the first airplane
William S. Gilbert	Orville Wright	Apple computers

Activity 8

Stephen Wozniak was a computer wizard who considered his innovation a gadget that would be of interest only to computer hobbiests like himself. Which of the following is therefore true? (More than one answer is possible).

1. Wozniak was exceptionally skilled in computer design.
2. Wozniak was motivated by financial profit.
3. Wozniak wanted to sell his computer to people in big business.
4. Wozniak thought his computer would be of most interest to people who enjoyed working with computers for fun and relaxation.

Activity 9

Describe the relationship between each of the following pairs of words (antonyms, synonyms, neither).

1. massive/small
2. cumbersome/awkward
3. expertise/innovation
4. muted/bright
5. anticipate/foresee
6. inevitable/avoidable
7. venture/risk
8. skeptical/unfriendly
9. potential/ability
10. donate/loan
11. collaborated/worked together
12. genuine/insincere
13. devise/invent

Activity 10

Circle the word that appropriately completes each of the following sentences.

1. Whenever the inventor was working on an innovation, she (emerged from/withdrew to) her house because she didn't want to be disturbed.
2. The new computer program was (collaborated/devised) by the newest student in the class.
3. The executives bought a (cumbersome/portable) copy machine because they needed to take it to meetings.
4. The computer enthusiast devised a portable model that had several practical (applications/markets) for educators.
5. It was Wozniak's (expertise/skepticism) that made it possible for him to devise the first personal computer.
6. The government (loaned/donated) $100 million to the corporation, expecting it to be repaid with 12 percent interest.
7. The investors (anticipated/intimidated) the higher profits because of the activity in the stock market.
8. When computers are not working, it is (inevitable/avoidable) that work will be delayed.

Activity 11

Cross out the one word that does not have the same meaning as the other three words.

1. Everyone liked the computer salesman because he was (genuine/calculating/sincere/unaffected).
2. The corporation president (benefited/contributed/gave/donated) his services to the school of business.
3. The sudden decrease in sales was not (understood/foreseen/anticipated/predicted) by anyone.
4. The corporate office of the manufacturing company was so close to the factory that the noise in the office was (muted/vivid/intense/extreme).
5. There are many specialized (parts/components/contributers/elements) in the memory bank of a computer.
6. The software company has the (capacity/extent/potential/ability) to employ 500 people.
7. After the young investor earned a million dollars, he was highly regarded for his financial (skillfulness/wizardry/good fortune/aptitude).
8. The software engineer's (expertise/intelligence/proficiency/mastery) was limited to one area.
9. The computer-game business (celebrated/thrived/prospered/progressed) during the summer months.
10. They undertook their (venture/risky undertaking/challenge/decision) after making careful calculations.

Activity 12

Some words have more than one form for a single part of speech. For example, "inventor" and "invention" are both noun forms; the different endings indicate different meanings. For each of the words listed below, find a noun that means "a person who . . ." The first one is done for you.

1. invention . . . inventor
2. innovation
3. investment
4. astronomy
5. expertise
6. technology
7. collaborate
8. wizardry
9. psychology
10. inheritance
11. mathematics

What endings did you find that can indicate "a person who . . ."?

Activity 13

Many irregular verbs appear as part of a more complex verb form. Complete the following chart, following the example.

Present Tense	Past Tense	Participle
1. oversee	oversaw	overseen
2. foresee		
3. overeat		
4. undertake		
5. mistake		
6. mislead		
7. uphold		
8. withhold		

(Other examples: undereat, overcome, undergo, underpay, overpay, overdo, outdo, overrun, overtake, foretell, outshine, overhang, override, oversleep, undersleep.)

Activity 14

Each underlined word is an inflected form of a base word. When you need to look up the word in the dictionary, you must look for the base form. In the blank before each sentence, indicate the form of the underlined word that you would look for in your dictionary. Follow the example.

_____shine_____ 1. The 18-year-old boy <u>outshone</u> his younger brother by winning a scholarship to a prestigious university.

_____ 2. I wish that I had <u>foreseen</u> the seriousness of the problem.

_____ 3. Although the computer programmer felt that he was <u>underpaid</u>, he remained in his job because computers were like a hobby to him.

_____ 4. I felt that I had been <u>misled</u> by the computer salesman when I discovered that my computer was not a state-of-the-art PC.

_____ 5. The man always gave his weekly paycheck to his wife, but he <u>withheld</u> $200 for himself.

_____ 6. When the president refused to approve the law, the law-makers <u>overrode</u> his decision.

_____ 7. I <u>mistook</u> you for your sister because you look alike.

Activity 15

A modifier can be formed by combining a noun with a past participle. It then becomes a compound adjective. Use your knowledge of the two words to define the following underlined compound adjectives. The first one is done for you.

1. He is seeking a computer-related career.

   a career that is related to computers

2. Typewriter-sized computers became available in the 1970s to replace the room-sized computers of the 1960s.

3. Children tend to like sugar-based cereals.

4. Whereas an integrated circuit is thumbnail-sized, the vacuum tubes in earlier computers were cigar-sized.

5. We are shopping for a precision-built car.

6. They lived near a tree-edged lake.

7. Jobs and Wozniak were self-taught computer experts.

Activity 16

In pairs or small groups, discuss each of the following questions.

1. Imagine that you just moved into an empty house. What can you use for a makeshift table? a makeshift pillow? a makeshift hammer?

2. Here are five gadgets found in many kitchens. Describe the functions of each: can opener, ice crusher, apple peeler, cheese grater. Name some other gadgets that are found in many kitchens.

3. If you were to design a state-of-the-art product, how would you improve the following products: toothbrush, bathtub, notebook, hairbrush?

4. Which of the following do you find intimidating? Why?

a teacher	a large truck on the road
a policeman	an automatic bank teller
a school counselor	a telephone-answering machine

5. What marketing techniques would you use if you wanted to sell a new soft drink product? What market would you focus on?

6. Which would be preferable for each of the following buildings, muted colors or bright? Why?

a restaurant	a post office	a hospital
a high school	a music store	a day-care center

7. What are the components of each of the following: a good marriage? a modern kitchen? a good stereo system?

8. Describe another entrepreneur whose investments led to fame and fortune.

9. Which of the following might be advertised as "state of the art?"

VCR	dictionary	washing machine
bread	antique vase	contact lenses
car		compact disc player

10. Under what circumstances does a business thrive? a tree? a young child? a marriage?

11. Name a notable pioneer in each of the following fields.

manufacturing	science	art
architecture	medicine	social services

12. What is a practical application of the personal computer in business? in the home?

PUTTING WORDS INTO SENTENCES

Ten words have been selected from the original vocabulary list for closer study. These words and their related forms are charted below.

Verbs	Nouns	Adjectives/ Participles	Adverbials
anticipate	anticipation	(un)anticipated anticipating	in anticipation of
collaborate	collaboration collaborator	collaborated	collaboratively
devise	device	devised	
emerge	emergence	emerging emergent	
foresee	foresight	(un)foreseen (un)foreseeable	(un)foreseeably
innovate	innovation innovator innovativeness	innovative	
intimidate	intimidation	(un)intimidating intimidated	
market	market marketability	marketable marketing	
thrive		thriving	
venture	venture	venturesome ventured	

Activity 1

Write a sentence of comparison using all of the words that are given. You may not change the word order. For example:

> typewriter/less/intimidating/computer
>
> *Many people think that the typewriter is less intimidating than the computer.*

1. the vacuum tubes of the 1950s/cumbersome/the integrated circuits of the 1970s.
2. Martin Alpert/venturesome/most people
3. The Apple I/marketable/earlier computers
4. Computer hobbiests/intimidated/the general public
5. Cumbersome computers/intimidating/portable computers

Activity 2

Restate the numbered sentences using the word forms below. You may need to add words or change the word order to make the sentences logical.

As technology advanced, the price of personal computers decreased and the market for them increased. (**a**) The first commercially available computer, the Univac I, was introduced to the public in 1951 and cost $2.5 million. (**b**) At this price its marketability was limited to governments and large businesses. (**c**) By 1980 a computer with comparable calculating capabilities could be purchased for $500, and it was routinely marketed to small businesses. (**d**) As the price progressively decreased, computer companies marketed their products to be used in schools and homes. (**e**) By the late 1980s, the computer market included most of the American public.

1. (Sentence **a**) marketed [verb]
2. (Sentence **b**) marketable
3. (Sentence **c**) market [noun]
4. (Sentence **d**) marketable
5. (Sentence **e**) marketed [verb]

The word <u>market</u> has become very useful in many business-related contexts. Following are some of the popular related usages:

> a buyer's market: a situation favoring a buyer.
> a seller's market: a situation favoring a seller.

> This is a good time to buy a new house because it is a buyer's market and the prices are low, but it's a bad time to sell a house because it is not a seller's market.

in the market for: seeking to buy.
on the market: for sale.

> I was in the market for a car, and I noticed that my friend had one on the market.

---

market value: the amount that can be obtained for goods or services on the open market.

The market value for produce fluctuates with the seasons.

stock market: the place where stocks and bonds are sold or the exchange of stocks and bonds.

He invested his inheritance in the stock market.

Activity 3

Imagine you were the chairman of the board of a small computer company in 1976. The personal computer has just been introduced by Apple Computers, and you want more information about the potential of this innovation. To gain the information you need, what questions would you ask your board members? Use each of the given words in a question. For example:

how/market

How has the computer market changed since last year?

1. where/market (noun)
2. where/market (verb)
3. why/more marketable
4. how/marketability/business community
5. is/market (noun)
6. will/marketing strategies

Activity 4

Restate each of the following sentences, using one of the words from the list. Use at least one word in each new sentence, making sure to use all of the words in the list. Change the word forms as needed.

collaborate	market	emerge
anticipate	devise	venture

1. Scientists have recently created a new testing procedure for heart disease.
2. They expect the new test to have far-reaching success.
3. Two German physicians have worked together to create the new test.
4. Evidence has come forth that indicates that this procedure may help limit the seriousness of heart disease for patients in the future.
5. Although the initial risk was costly, the results will be ultimately worthwhile.

Activity 5

Restate the following sentences using the word forms below. You may need to add words or change the word order to make the sentences logical.

(a) America's pioneers of high technology may have put men on the moon, but their creativity hasn't solved every problem. (b) Purely technological innovations have not solved many critical sociological problems such as food shortages. (c) This challenge is now being addressed by some innovators who are trying to be more sensitive to the people and the environment. (d) For example, an elaborate innovation that works well for an Iowa farmer can be useless for most farmers who till soil in underdeveloped countries. (e) What these farmers need is some innovative "low" technology—such as an improved plow that can be pulled by a water buffalo. (f) More of industry's innovative energy needs to be spent on improving the human condition.

1. (Sentence a) innovativeness
2. (Sentence b) innovators
3. (Sentence c) innovativeness
4. (Sentence d) innovative
5. (Sentence e) innovation
6. (Sentence f) innovators

Activity 6

To anticipate something has more than one meaning, one of which is similar to and may be interchanged with *to foresee* something.

> The stockbroker *(foresaw/anticipated)* the problems in the market and withdrew his funds before he lost money.
> The stockbroker *(foresaw/anticipated)* that the market would have problems, and he withdrew his funds before he lost money.

Read the paragraph, then restate the sentences, using the words forms below. You may need to add words or change the word order to make the sentence logical.

(a) One of the results of the electronics revolution that was not expected was that many people began to leave the workplace and to run businesses from their homes. (b) Even when the number of home professionals totaled nine million in 1987, the experts didn't anticipate that the increase would continue. (c) Some of the home entrepreneurs had left their jobs because of the expectation of corporation cost-cutting; (d) they had known they would lose their jobs. (e) Although the start-up costs for home businesses are often higher than home professionals expect, (f) other savings may not be anticipated. (g) For example, one businesswoman said that she would save at least $2,000 a year because she would not have to drive to work, go out to lunch as often, buy as many dressy chothes, or pay for cleaning bills.

1. (Sentence a) unforeseen result
2. (Sentence b) unanticipated
3. (Sentence c) anticipated (verb)
4. (Sentence d) foreseen (adj.)
5. (Sentence e) unanticipated
6. (Sentence f) unforeseen
7. (Sentence g) the anticipated savings

Activity 7

A *venture* is an enterprise that involves risk or speculation.

The entrepreneurs put all their money in the business venture.

When used as a verb, *to venture* can be either transitive or intransitive.

You shouldn't venture all of your money on one investment.

Don't venture too near the edge of the cliff.

Following are the figures tracing the investments of three very successful entrepreneurs. Use this information to write sentences that incorporate the listed words.

Apple Computers

Investor	Investment	Shareholdings in 1981
Steven Jobs	$1300 in 1976 (joint investment: Jobs and Wozniak)	$165 million
Stephen Wozniak		$88 million
A.C. Markkula	$250,000 in 1977	$154 million
Mike Scott	his career; he took a 50 percent pay cut to become president of the the company in 1977	$62 million

1. A.C. Markula/ventured/Apple Computers
2. Jobs and Wozniak's/venture (noun)/earned
3. investment/more venturesome
4. Mike Scott/ventured

Activity 8

Read the pararaph, then restate the sentences, using the word forms below. You may need to add words or change the word forms to make the sentences logical.

William R. Hewlett and David Packard studied electrical engineering together at Stanford University in the 1930s. (**a**) Because they were such promising students, they were encouraged by their professors to work together to start their own company. (**b**) At first they were hesitant to begin the new company because of the Depression, but these two young men were too confident to be easily discouraged. (**c**) Since they began working together in 1939, their business has been one of the most successful in the Silicon Valley. (**d**) The two men have been a solid team; both men share all technical and organizational responsibilities. (**e**) Although their first manufacturing plant was a makeshift operation in Packard's garage, they were unafraid to market their products in some of the largest companies in the nation. (**f**) Fifty years after the first joint effort of these two men, the firm of Hewlett-Packard has become one of the most admired electronics corporations in the world, showing that two heads can at times be better than one.

1. (Sentence **a**) collaborate
2. (Sentence **b**) intimidated
3. (Sentence **c**) collaborators
4. (Sentence **d**) collaboratively
5. (Sentence **e**) unintimidated (adj.)
6. (Sentence **f**) collaborated
7. (Sentence **f**) collaboration

Activity 9

Reread the paragraphs in Activities 2 and 8 of this chapter. Then answer the questions that follow, using the words in parentheses in your answers.

1. When did William R. Hewlett and David Packard first become known as successful businessmen? (emerged)
2. Was their business successful when it first became public in 1939? (emergence)
3. When did the UNIVAC I first appear on the market? (emerged)
4. Was the introduction of the UNIVAC I accompanied by immediate success in small business? (emergence)

USING WORDS IN CONTEXT

Activity 1

Complete the paragraph below.

      Although Jobs and Wozniak have become known as two of the most brilliant innovators in the technological revolution, not all of their (1) _____ were as successful as the Apple I and the Apple II. They (2) _____ the Apple II Plus in 1980 when they (3) _____ that small businesses would have a need for a more professional and integrated system than the Apple I or II. The Apple II Plus was an advanced version of the Apple II that they aimed at the small business (4) _____. Unfortunately, they did not (5) _____ the competition of the IBM Personal Computer. Although IBM was not the original (6) _____ of the personal computer, they had been the leader in the business machine industry for several decades, and they soon (7) _____ as the primary competition in the personal computer (8) _____. IBM had many advantages over Apple: their engineering was done by a more experienced engineering staff, and their advertising was done by their more experienced (9) _____ staff. Since Apple had been so successful with the Apple I and the Apple II, the failure of their (10) _____ with the Apple II Plus was both (11) _____ and disappointing.

Activity 2

Your instructor will dictate a paragraph about another invention of Steven Jobs and Stephen Wozniak. After you have written the paragraph, work with a partner to fill in words you may have missed or to correct grammar and spelling. When you and your partner believe your paragraphs are correct, compare them to the the paragraph printed at the back of the book. Make any necessary corrections.

Activity 3

The space program was established to investigate the mysteries of the solar system, but many of its technological discoveries have improved life for people on earth as well.

Invention	Function on Earth
Carbon monoxide monitor	measures pollution in cities
Dirt analyzer	identifies poisons in humans through blood analysis
Heated space suit	protective clothing for construction workers
Miniature seismometer	helps predict earthquakes
Horizontal shower	bathes bedridden patients
Control switch that allows immobilized astronauts to operate controls by eye motion	enables paralyzed patients to control television, book page turners, bed position, lights, etc.

1. With a partner or small group, take turns describing some of the benefits to daily life that have been received from the space program. Do not write your sentences. The various forms of the following words may help you express your ideas: innovation, device, pioneer, anticipate, foresee, emerge, potential, state-of-the-art, applications.

2. In your opinion, which of the above inventions provides the greatest benefit for people on earth? Write a paragraph which explains your choice.

Activity 4

Look in the business section of a newspaper. Find an article about a business venture (a new company, a failing venture, an expanding company, a changing business, etc.)

1. Read the article and underline any words that you studied in this chapter.
2. Prepare to describe this venture in class, summarizing the article for your classmates. You may find varying forms of the following words useful: anticipate, collaborate, devise, foresee, market, pioneer, entrepreneur, expertise, innovation, investment, potential, technology, venture, state-of-the-art, thereby, whereas.

Activity 5

Imagine that you were a journalist for a local newspaper in the Silicon Valley in 1986. Reynold B. Johnson was just awarded the National Medal of Technology by President Reagan and you were assigned the task of writing a brief article about his life and accomplishments. Use the following notes to write your article. You may find the following words useful: venture, devise, market, pioneer, expertise, potential, technology, state-of-the-art, thereby, whereas, application.

Personal information: Born—Minnesota (1906)
                         Childhood—rural
                         Parents—farmers
Educational information: University of Minnesota
Professional information:
    Taught science and math—Michigan High School (1931)
    Invented electric test-score machine (1932)
    Worked at IBM (1934–1971)
    Granted 84 patents (1934–1971)
    Invented the magnetic disc (makes stored information directly available for computer processing. Made possible such operations as airline reservation systems, inventory management, automated banking, space flights, and word processing).

Activity 6

Read the following paragraph as many times as you can in three minutes. Then with your book closed, rewrite as much of the information as you can remember.

By 1987 the computer market on American college campuses was thriving. Sales people from all the personal computer companies were actively pursuing the business of college administrators, professors, and students. They were selling computers for less than half price and were adding attractive bonuses such as free software and support services. They were willing to venture a great deal of time and money in this market because they foresaw that it would thrive for a long time. There are 14 million people who provide or receive education on campuses, including 2.5 million new freshmen every year. Students who buy computers are likely to become lifetime customers who may enter business after graduation and influence corporate buying decisions.

Topics for Writing or Discussion

1. Describe a kitchen gadget that you think should be invented. What would it do? Who would buy it? How should it be marketed?

2. Imagine that you are the computer shop owner who bought the first model of the personal computer from Jobs and Wozniak. Why were you interested, and what did you anticipate from this venture? Use the facts from the article as a framework for your story. How do you plan to market it? To whom will you market it? What makes you willing to take this venture?

3. How has the world benefited from the invention of the personal computer? What problems have accompanied the computer revolution?

4. Of all the advantages that the computer has brought to the modern world, which is the most beneficial?

5. Describe the invention that has had the greatest effect on the 20th century.

5

THE STORY OF MOTION PICTURES

ESTABLISHING A CONTEXT

Pre-reading Discussion

- What makes a motion picture great? What great motion pictures can you name?
- In what ways does a motion picture resemble a novel? In what ways is it different?
- How have motion pictures changed since they were first invented?

> Read this article for general meaning. If you cannot understand the meaning of the content, use a dictionary to look up key words (words that are important to the meaning).

(1)   The theater darkens, and the audience quiets in anticipation as the screen in front of them comes alive with pictures and sound. A story is about to be conveyed through the medium of motion pictures. As the screen story unfolds, the audience becomes engrossed in the drama, unaware of the many narrative devices employed in the film to make the story comprehensible. To fully appreciate how these storytelling devices are used in film making, it is necessary to know something of the history of motion pictures and of the principles of film production.

(2)   Motion pictures were introduced to the public in 1894, with the invention of a cumbersome viewing machine. Inside the machine, a mechanism conveyed a short strip of film past a viewing window. By carefully controlling the speed at which the film was conveyed, the machine created the illusion that the photographs were moving. For a few cents, people could peek into the machine and see a short film. They were fascinated. Envisioning a profit, entrepreneurs installed hundreds of viewing machines in hotels, stores, and restaurants. However, their investment in these sensational gadgets was high, and their profits were small because only one person at a time could be entertained. Entrepreneurs had visions of a machine that could project enlarged images of the moving pictures onto a wall so that one machine could entertain many people simultaneously.

Actors in silent films, such as those in this scene from a Charlie Chaplin movie, had to exaggerate their gestures and facial expressions.

(3)   Their dream was realized with Thomas Edison's invention of the motion picture projector. Its appearance in 1896 made possible the exhibition of films to large audiences, and soon theaters that had previously featured only live entertainment began exhibiting a sequence of one-minute soundless films between the singers, dancers, and trained dog acts. The films were an immediate sensation. Especially popular were films of runaway horses, rushing fire engines, marching parades, and crashing ocean waves. Although these films were nothing more than photographs of familiar scenes, audiences, dazzled by the visual wizardry, inundated theater owners with requests for new films. Film makers easily dealt with this demand: a camera operator merely went outdoors and photographed anything interesting he saw. The scene he photographed was precisely what the audience eventually saw in the theater.

(4)   It soon became increasingly difficult to find interesting new scenes to film, but inventive movie makers overcame the problem by hiring actors to perform scenes for the camera. A scene, in film terminology, is an event that occurs in one place and at one time. When the place or time of the action changes, the scene is over. Since these early movies comprised only one scene, the plots were simple. Frequently they depicted a daring rescue from a dangerous situation. Longer films were created by putting two or three scenes together. For instance, a film might include a scene of a child in a burning house, a scene of a rushing fire engine, and a scene of a fireman subsequently rescuing the child.

(5)   Film storytelling took a revolutionary leap forward with the 1904 film *The Great Train Robbery*. Composed of fourteen scenes that lasted a total of 12 minutes, this western film, complete with horses and gunfighting, was far longer than any previous film. However, what distinguished this motion picture from earlier films was not just its greater length, but the effective story it was able to project by employing the simple yet innovative technique of editing. After the scenes of the robbery, the chase, and the capture had been photographed on film, the film was edited by literally cutting apart the successive scenes of the story and rearranging them in a new, more effective sequence. The story begins with a scene in a railroad telegraph office. The robbers enter and tie up the telegraph operator. After they rob the train, the action returns to the telegraph office, where the telegraph operator is now struggling to untie himself. What emerged from the edited version of the film was a dramatic, exciting story. *The Great Train Robbery* introduced an important principle of motion picture narration: the sequence of the scenes in relation to each other helps create an effective story.

(6)   Film makers soon discovered how difficult it was to tell a coherent story with pictures alone. Since early motion pictures were ''silent,'' narration depended almost entirely on the actions of the film actors. If their actions were not clear, the audience would not be able to comprehend the story. For this reason, the actors greatly exaggerated their body movements, gestures, and facial expressions. Costumes and sets (movie locations) also helped narrate. A funny hat, a ragged dress, or a battlefield reflected the personality or circumstances of a screen character, and therefore served a narrative function by helping the audience understand the story.

(7)   As pioneer film makers attempted longer and more complex stories, they were concerned that audiences might not be able to follow the plot. This prompted them to create additional narrative devices to make film stories comprehensible. For example, new camera techniques were employed. Instead of the camera remaining stationary with the action moving in front of it, the camera itself moved to focus on parts of a scene. An amusing scene in a restaurant might show a shot, or view, of a man eating soup, then a shot of a woman eating soup, then a close-up shot of a spider falling into one of their bowls. The close-up focuses the audience's attention on something significant in the story. In this scene, perhaps the man will try to flirt with the woman as the spider crawls up his spoon. A long-distance shot serves a different narrative function. It often establishes the place where the subsequent action will occur. For example, a long-distance shot of a prison suggests that the next scene will occur inside the prison.

(8)   Lighting can also contribute to the narration. Degrees of dark and light can project a mood of danger, sadness, or romance. Gradually diminishing light at the end of a scene, called a fade-out in film terminology, serves as a clear transition between two scenes separated in time. In fact, many narrative devices function to clarify the time element in movies. Because the events in a story might take place over days, weeks, or even years, film makers had to create visual devices to express chronology. Showing the turning hands of a clock or the changing pages of a calendar is one way to depict the passage of time. In contrast, a film can create the illusion of simultaneous events by interrupting a scene with other action and then returning to the original scene. Cross-cutting back and forth between shots of the pursued and shots of the pursuer is a common technique in chase scenes. Narrative devices such as these make a film story comprehensible and coherent. That is, they help audiences understand the sequence of events by combining the separate scenes into a unified story.

(9)   As motion pictures improved in the early 1900s, they became increasingly popular. To keep pace with the public's demand for films, makeshift motion picture theaters were set up in empty stores and offices, sometimes as many as five to a city block. For a nickel, theater-goers could see comedy, drama, adventure, and romance while a piano player provided music appropriate to the action on the screen: touching music for sad scenes, exhilarating music for chase scenes, and so on. Although independent of the film itself, the musical accompaniment enhanced the film narration by creating a mood.

(10)   In fact, music was so critical to screen narration that film makers began experimenting with ways to synchronize recorded music with films. By the late 1920s they had devised a way to include music on the filmstrip itself. They never intended that films should ''talk,'' but in *The Jazz Singer*, the first words in a motion picture were spoken. Within a few years, all films talked, and films were able to narrate a story not just with pictures and music, but with dialogue and sound effects synchronized with the screen action.

(11)   Supplementing pictures with sound gave films a richness of new narrative tools. Like a close-up shot, a sound could focus the audience's attention on something significant. Sound effects could also reveal the time and place of a scene or create a mood. For example, a crowing rooster suggested morning in the country, and a howling wind on a dark night made terrified audiences shiver in fear. Bells rang, crowds cheered, and guns exploded. But the most significant impact of sound was that actors could talk.

(12)   The addition of dialogue to motion pictures revolutionized not only the way that film stories were narrated but also the kinds of stories that could be told on film. Stories that had been virtually impossible to narrate through pictures alone could now be effectively narrated through pictures and sound. Through dialogue, characters could reveal critical information about the plot, about themselves, or about other characters. Dialogue could also be used to explain past events or anticipate future action.

(13)   After films could talk, many popular novels, short stories, and classic literary works were adapted for the screen. Dialogue from literature was often literally transferred to the screen version of a story, but descriptions had to be rewritten. If a description could be represented visually, then the camera told the story. If a description could not be represented visually, then the dialogue told the story. For example, an author might write, "Distressed that they would miss their airplane flight, Jim and Ann quickly packed their suitcases and rushed out of the hotel room, not realizing that they had left their airline tickets on the table."

(14)   The filming plan might look something like this:

Scene 27: Interior of hotel room.   Time: 14 seconds.

Camera	Action	Dialogue
medium-shot	Jim opens door.	Hurry! The plane leaves in 15 mintues!
	Ann closes suitcase.	We've got to make it!
	They hurry out.	
close-up	Tickets on table.	
fade-out		

(15)   Before the production of a movie can begin, the motion picture director, who coordinates every aspect of filming, carefully plans each scene in collaboration with the writer of the screen story. Together they visualize how to divide the story into scenes and what each scene will contribute to the development of the story. Then the director establishes a filming schedule, for the scenes are usually not filmed chronologically. As each scene is filmed, the director collaborates with a team of technical experts, including the lighting technician, the sound technician, the camera operator, the set designer, and the costume designer. Most important, the director collaborates with the actors themselves to establish how they will portray their film characters. The director is guided by an important principle of good film making: every element in the film—the lighting, the costumes, the dialogue—has a function in narrating the film story.

(16)   After the dozens of scenes are filmed and edited in their final form, sound effects and mood music are added to the sound track. If the film makers have done their jobs well, the result will be an entertaining story told through the medium of motion pictures.

Comprehension Check

The purpose of this activity is to check your understanding of the article and to give practice using vocabulary words. Label each sentence true or false according to the article. If you cannot understand the meaning of a sentence, use a dictionary to look up key words.

1. Thomas Edison's projector made it possible for many people to see live performers simultaneously.

2. Actors in silent films would exaggerate their facial expressions to help make the story comprehensible.
3. *The Great Train Robbery* revolutionized movie production by being the first film to employ dialogue.
4. Screen storywriters adapt popular novels for the medium of motion pictures.
5. A scene comprises a sequence of events that take place chronologically over days, weeks, or even years.
6. Silent film makers envisioned films in which actors could reveal critical information about the plot through dialogue.
7. Films employ visual devices to depict the passage of time.
8. The illusion of motion is created when a film strip is conveyed through a motion picture projector.
9. Music can enhance the mood created by film actions.
10. The function of a close-up shot is to focus the attention of the audience on something amusing in the plot.

UNDERSTANDING WORDS

Vocabulary List

Verbs	Nouns	Adjectives/ Participles	Adverbials
adapt	expression	coherent	chronologically
comprise	illusion	comprehensible	literally
convey	medium	critical	simultaneously
create	mood	dramatic	
depict	sensation	effective	
employ	sequence	live	
enhance	version	popular	
envision		visual	
exaggerate			
exhibit			
focus			
perform			
project			
realize			
reveal			
revolutionize			

Subject-Specific Vocabulary

Nouns: dialogue, film, scene, plot.　　**Adjective:** narrative.

Activity 1

Circle the one word or phrase that does not have the same meaning as the other three.

1. Early films often (consisted of/contained/comprised/conveyed) one scene that (showed/depicted/represented/created) a daring rescue.

2. Pioneer film makers (created/invented/performed/devised) new narrative devices to make film plots more (coherent/visual/connected/unified).

3. Silent film actors had to (express/project/send/adapt) their emotions clearly when they (acted/exaggerated/played/performed) in a dramatic scene.

4. Film entrepreneurs (imagined/envisioned/dreamed of/developed) recorded music played simultaneously with the film action.

5. Muted lighting (reveals/adds to/enhances/strengthens) the (emotion/feeling/mood/plot) in sad scenes.

6. Silent films often (used/employed/adapted/utilized) printed captions between scenes to make the plots (clear/exciting/comprehensible/understandable).

7. Sound effects can (focus/center/concentrate/reveal) the audience's attention on a detail that is (critical/important/interesting/essential) to the plot.

8. Through dialogue, film detectives can (expose/explain/discover/reveal) how they solved a mystery.

9. The first lavish theater built in the 1920s to (convey/exhibit/show/display) motion pictures was (a cause of excitement/a hit/an expense/a sensation).

10. As a state-of-the-art entertainment medium, television (enhanced/revolutionized/changed/altered) the entertainment industry and caused a (marked/striking/temporary/dramatic) drop in movie attendance.

11. The approval of film reviewers can be (critical/essential/effective/important) to a film's success and can (actually/really/virtually/literally) determine its future.

Activity 2

Substitute a word or a form of a word from the vocabulary list for each word or phrase in parentheses. Be sure to keep the meaning of the original sentences.

Motion pictures do not literally move. The (visual trick) of motion is (made) by the motion picture projector and the viewer's eye. A motion picture film strip (contains) a (series) of still photographs, each one slightly different from the one it follows. When the filmstrip is (moved) in front of a rapidly flashing light in the projector, the pictures in the photographs appear to move. The (visual trick) of motion also depends on the physical principle called "the persistence of vision." This means that the eye retains a (sight) image for a fraction of a second after the view itself has disappeared and while a new view is appearing. This has the effect of the eye seeing two images (at the same time). As the images merge, they give the illusion of motion.

An optical illusion is a visual trick. Here is a well-known optical illusion. Which line is longer, line A or line B?

Of course they are the same length, but the out-pointing lines at the ends of B visually extend B, creating the illusion that it is longer than A.

Activity 3

Popular stories are told again and again, sometimes in new versions. For example, Shakespeare's classic play *Romeo and Juliet* might be performed in a modern version, a comedy version, a musical version, a film version, a shortened version, or a foreign language version. Match each of these terms with one of the descriptions below.

1. The play is adapted for motion pictures.
2. The actors sing their words.
3. The old-fashioned language is changed to present-day language.
4. The dialogue includes many jokes.
5. The words have been translated into another language.
6. Just some of the scenes are included.

Activity 4

Adopt and *adapt* are frequently confused. *To adopt* means "to take possession of something as one's own." *To adapt* means "to change something to fit a particular purpose." For example:

> *The immigrant adapted to living in his adopted land.*
> *A couple that adopts a baby must adapt to being parents.*

Use *adopt* or *adapt* in each sentence below.

1. Actors frequently _____ a new name when they enter show business.

2. Film actors may find it difficult to _____ to acting live on a stage.

3. When you enter a dark theater, it takes a few moments for your eyes to _____ to the dark.

4. Teenagers often _____ the hairstyles of their favorite rock singers.

Activity 5

Verbs of emotion have two adjective forms, one that expresses the cause of the emotion and one that expresses the emotional effect. For example:

> Monsters *frighten* people. (verb = frighten)
> The *frightened* audience shrieked as the *frightening* film monster destroyed New York. (adjectives = frightened/frightening)

In most cases, the cause form ends in -ing and the effect form ends in -ed. Since the effect is an emotion, it can be used to describe only living beings (usually human), since only living beings can experience emotions.

> *Jack fell asleep during the boring movie.*

Although the sentence does not say it, we know how Jack felt. He felt bored. The boring movie caused the emotion. In the article, find the adjective forms of these verbs of emotion. For each word, tell who felt the emotion and what caused the emotion. The paragraph numbers are given in parentheses. For example:

> engross (paragraph 1)

> *The audience was engrossed.*
> *The drama was engrossing.*

1. fascinate (2)	4. amuse (7)	7. terrify (11)
2. dazzle (3)	5. exhilarate (9)	8. distress (13)
3. excite (5)	6. touch (9)	9. entertain (16)

Not all cause adjectives end in -ing. Check your dictionary for the two adjective forms of these verbs: impress, scare, delight.

Activity 6

To depict something is to represent it in words or pictures. *To perform* something is to do it. *To exhibit* something is to show it. Use a form of *depict, perform* or *exhibit* in each space below. In some spaces, more than one word may be correct.

The original Superman was a cartoon hero who _____ supernatural powers and _____ sensational deeds to save the world from evil. The cartoons _____ him as strong, handsome, and unaffected by the charms of Lois Lane, a newspaper reporter in love with him. When the Superman stories were adapted for films, the role of Superman was _____ by several different actors over the years. Superman's daring deeds had been easy to _____ in cartoons, but required special effects to _____ on the screen. Like the original cartoon Superman, the modern film Superman _____ deeds requiring great strength. But Superman films of today _____ the hero as having more human emotions. And for the first time, he reveals his love for Lois Lane.

Activity 7

1. When a paragraph, a story, or a film is coherent, all of its parts fit together logically to form a unified whole. Rearrange these sentences into a coherent paragraph.
   a. Soon audiences began to recognize the faces of certain actors that they liked.
   b. In early films, the names of the actors were not revealed.
   c. A popular actor virtually assured a film's success.
   d. As a result, film makers started promoting their films by advertising the names of the actors.

2. Add words or phrases to make the paragraph coherent. There are many possible choices.

Many problems were involved in the production of early sound films. _____ the camera was so noisy that its sounds were recorded along with the voices of the actors. _____ the camera was padded with heavy cloth. _____ the camera became so cumbersome that it literally could not be moved. _____ not all actors had appropriate voices for sound films. _____ some had heavy foreign accents or high, squeaky voices.

Activity 8

To enhance something is to make it better or more effective. To exaggerate something is to make it seem greater than it is in reality.

> Black eye make-up exaggerates the eyes.
> Muted eye make-up enhances the color of the eyes.

Use a form of exaggerate or enhance in each sentence.

1. Wearing too much make-up _____ facial wrinkles.
2. An appropriate picture frame _____ the beauty of a painting.
3. Realistic art depicts objects as they really are; abstract art often _____ the size or color of an object.
4. Color film _____ the sense of reality in nature movies.
5. Appreciation of the arts can _____ your life.

> To exaggerate (without a following object) means to overstate or tell more than the truth.
>
> JOHNNY: Mommy! You should have seen the big fish I caught! It must have been a hundred feet long!
> MOTHER: Johnny, I've told you a million times not to exaggerate.

Activity 9

A motion picture comprises several scenes. What do the art forms on the left comprise? Match the art form with the parts that it comprises. Use a dictionary to look up unfamiliar words.

a symphony	cartoons
a play	steps
a dance	stanzas
a poem	chapters
a comic strip	acts
a novel	movements

Activity 10

Science fiction films have depicted many technological and scientific developments that have later been realized (become real). Which of these creations of science fiction have been realized?

> people journey to the moon in a spaceship
> cities are built under the ocean
> robots perform work in factories
> doctors transplant human brains
> automobiles are equipped with telephones

A more common meaning of *to realize* is ''to learn suddenly'' or ''to be aware of.''

> *I read half of the book before I realized that I had read it before.*

Activity 11

Motion pictures are both a visual art and a performance art. In the list below, put a **V** before each visual art and a **P** before each performance art.

ballet	drawing	painting
singing	sculpture	playing the piano

Activity 12

Arrange the following imaginary newspaper headlines chronologically.

TALKING MOVIES POPULAR WITH AUDIENCES

EDISON INVENTS MOVIE PROJECTOR

THE GREAT TRAIN ROBBERY REVOLUTIONIZES FILMS

VIEWING MACHINES ARE NEWEST U.S. SENSATION

INVENTORS ENVISION WAY TO RECORD MUSIC ON FILM

Activity 13

To *convey* something has two meanings. One is "to carry something from one place to another." The second is "to communicate something." Complete each sentence with an appropriate word or phrase.

1. _____ convey people from place to place in shopping malls.

2. _____ convey knowledge to students.

3. Businesses use _____ to convey information from one office to another.

4. People send _____ to convey holiday greetings to their friends.

Activity 14

Below is a list of various communication media (the plural of *medium*). Identify them in several ways.

cartoon	poster	opera	magazine
television	stage play	radio	motion picture
newspaper	novel	T-shirt	junk mail

1. Which are narrative media?
2. Which are news media?
3. Which are printed media?
4. Which are advertising media?

The term "the media" is used to refer to news media.

Activity 15

Discuss the following questions in pairs or small groups.

1. Two friends see a movie together. When the movie is over, one friend complains that he did not comprehend the movie. The other says it was completely comprehensible to her. What are some reasons why the film could be comprehensible to her and not to him?

2. What will be the results if each of these is effective: a low-calorie diet, an insect poison, a speed-reading class, a vacuum cleaner?

3. An advertisement sells a product by focusing on its desirable qualities, such as its good taste or the beauty that will result from its use. If you were creating an advertisement for a new toothpaste, what would you focus on? Who or what would you depict in your advertisement?

4. "The fire alarm rang and we rushed out to the school yard. A holiday mood prevailed as we waited for permission to return to our classrooms." How would stu-

dents in a holiday mood behave? "The interruption put our teacher in a bad mood for the rest of the day." How would someone in a bad mood behave?

5. Name some inventions of the last 100 years that have revolutionized communication. Which of these inventions do you think has had the most dramatic effect on society? Why?

6. What is meant by the expression "One picture is worth a thousand words"?

7. Add a word or phrase that contrasts with the word *live* in the following advertisements or announcements.

Outside a nightclub: LIVE MUSIC EVERY SATURDAY
_____ MUSIC SUNDAY THROUGH FRIDAY

In a market: Live plants $3.95
_____ plants $5.95

On the label of a cassette tape of concert music:
Recorded live.
Recorded _____

8. What synonyms are used in the article for the word *film*, as in the phrase "film writer"?

9. What machine, equipment, or instrument is critical to the jobs of each of these people: a photographer, a chef, a gardener, a physician?

PUTTING WORDS INTO SENTENCES

Ten words have been selected from the original vocabulary list for closer study. These words and their related forms are charted below.

Verbs	Nouns	Adjectives/Participles	Adverbials
create	creator		
	creation	creative	creatively
	creativity		
criticize	critic	critical	critically
	criticism		
dramatize	drama	dramatic	dramatically
effect	effect	effective	effectively
affect			
envision	vision	visual	visually
visualize	visionary	(in)visible	(in)visibly
express	expression	expressive	expressively
		express	expressly
	literature	literary	
	(il)literacy	(il)literate	
		literal	literally

Verbs	Nouns	Adjectives/ Participles	Adverbials
popularize	popularity	popular	popularly
sense	sensation	sensational	sensationally
	sense	sensitive	sensitively
	sensitivity		

Activity 1

One meaning of *sense* is an awareness or feeling. *To sense* something is to be aware of it or to perceive it.

> *We could sense that the audience liked the play.*

A *sensation* is also a feeling, but it is usually a bodily feeling rather than a mental or emotional feeling.

> *Descending in an elevator gives people the sensation of falling. They have the sensation of falling.*

A *sensation* can also refer to a person, object, or event of great interest or excitement. *Sensational*, the adjective form, has the added meaning "wonderful or terrific."

> The Jazz Singer *was a sensation.*
> *Al Jolson was sensational in the starring role.*

Change each of the sentences below to include the words *sense*, *sensed*, *sensation*, or *sensational*.

1. Movie makers of the 1950s were aware that they needed to create new kinds of films to lure people away from their TV sets and back to the movie theaters.
2. One attempt to do this was the 3D (three-dimensional) film, which gave audiences a feeling of reality by creating the illusion of depth in films.
3. Movie-goers could perceive this depth only by wearing special glasses.
4. The first 3D movies were very popular.
5. Audiences felt like they were actually in the movies.
6. The most exciting scenes were those that gave audiences the feeling of motion.
7. This feeling was so real that some people actually became seasick while watching scenes of boats.

<u>Sensationalism</u> refers to attempts by the media to create public interest by focusing on shocking subject matter or using shocking language.

> The Evening News *depends on sensationalism to sell newpapers.*

Activity 2

To have a sense of something means "to understand" something, "to be aware" of it, or "to appreciate" it.

> *Teachers need to have a good sense of humor. Mr. Reed, however, has no sense of humor.*

Some common phrases of this type are:

a sense of rhythm   a sense of color
a sense of direction   a sense of business

Reword each of these sentences to include *a sense of (noun)* or *no sense of (noun)*. The first one has been done for you.

1. Balance is important for dancers.

   > *Dancers must have a good sense of balance.*

2. Babies do not understand right and wrong.
3. The President felt he was responsible for the well-being of the country.
4. Artists feel proud when their works are exhibited.

We receive all information about the world through our five <u>senses</u>: sight, hearing, smell, taste, and touch. Some people claim they have a "sixth sense" or an "extra sense" that gives them special powers, such as being able to foresee the future. These special powers are referred to as Extra Sensory Perception, or ESP.

Activity 3

A *sensitive* person is one whose emotions are easily aroused, often in a negative way. It can also refer to a person or a thing that easily detects something. A *sensitive* topic is one that can cause uncomfortable emotions.

> *Don't mention his grey hair. He's sensitive about it.*
> *Bankers must be sensitive to changes in the economy.*

Sensitive can also describe a person or thing that exhibits gentle or delicate feelings about a subject.

> *On Golden Pond was a sensitive film about the fear of growing old.*

Restate the following sentences, using *sensitive, sensitively,* or *sensitivity*.

1. Television advertisers may be reluctant to sponsor a program that deals with controversial social issues.
2. If they do sponsor such a program, they may insist that the issue be portrayed delicately.

3. Television advertisers are also aware of the kinds of products they can advertise on television.

4. They know that viewers are very uncomfortable about discussing bodily functions, for example.

5. Therefore, personal hygiene products must be advertised with great care.

Activity 4

Look up the names of the following devices in a dictionary. Tell what each senses or what it is sensitive to.

smoke detector   Geiger counter
thermostat   seismograph

<u>To make sense</u> means "to be logical."
  When you're tired, it makes sense to go to bed.
  The explanation in the book doesn't make sense.

<u>Common sense</u> refers to thinking or behaving in a practical manner.
  Someone with common sense would remember to bring a pencil to an examination.

Activity 5

Restate each sentence, using one of these words: *create, creation, creator, creativity, creative,* or *creatively.*

1. A work of art is something that is much admired for its great beauty.

2. An artist can produce a work of art in music, poetry, photography, architecture, or in any other art medium.

3. Not all artists' products are works of art.

4. A work of art requires the artist to show inventiveness in the use of his or her medium.

5. That is, the artist must use the medium in a new and exciting way.

6. The product must be pleasing to the senses.

7. A work of art must effectively project the mood the artist intended to express.

8. Finally, a work of art makes a lasting impression and remains forever beautiful.

The Creator (written with a capital letter) refers to God.
  We are thankful to the Creator for the beauty of the world we live in.

Activity 6

The relationship between a creator and his/her creation may be stated in either active or passive form.

Walt Disney created Mickey Mouse. (active)
Mickey Mouse was created by Walt Disney. (passive)

Active forms emphasize the performer of the action. Passive forms emphasize the result of the action. Sometimes passive sentences do not even name the performer of the action if the performer is not significant or is unknown.

Mickey Mouse was created in 1928.

Only transitive verbs (those that have a following object) can occur in the passive form. Notice the verbs below.

The first Mickey Mouse cartoon failed because it was a silent film. (Failed has no following object.)
When the film studio added sound, the next cartoon was a box-office sensation. (Added is followed by an object, so the sentence can be made passive.)
When sound was added, the next cartoon was a box-office sensation.

In passive sentences, the verb becomes a form of *be* (is, are, was, were) that agrees with the sentence subject in number (singular or plural) and expresses the correct tense (present or past) plus the past participle of the main verb.

The cartoons were drawn in black and white until 1932.
Today Mickey Mouse is known around the world.

Create sentences, using the information below. Do not change the order of the information, but change the verb tense if necessary, or make the sentence passive.

1. Edgar Allan Poe	create	short stories and poems
2. *Tom Sawyer*	write	Mark Twain
3. television	invent	1920
4. The Beatles	popularize	rock music
5. Ernest Hemingway	win	Nobel Prize for literature
6. U.S. Civil War	dramatize	*Gone with the Wind*

Activity 7

An *expression* is an outward representation of an inner feeling. People use words, pictures, gestures, or other means to express how they feel.

Use the given word to describe these representations of feelings. The first one has been done for you.

1. thank you (to express)

   People say thank you to express gratitude.

2. a kiss (expression)

3. newspaper editorial (to express)
4. a national anthem (expresses)

Activity 8

Change these sentences to include the words *expressive* or *expressively*.

1. Martin Luther King's voice showed his feelings.

   He spoke expressively.
   He had an expressive voice.

2. Picasso's painting depicted his mood.

3. Charlie Chaplin used his eyes to show his emotions.

4. Poe wrote of his great love in the poem ''Annabel Lee.''

Activity 9

Express (adjective) can also mean ''clear, precise or special.'' *Expressly* means ''clearly or especially.'' Change each of these sentences to include *express* or *expressly*.

1. Violence is often shown in films for the precise intent of shocking audiences.

   Violence is often shown for the express purpose of shocking audiences.
   Violence is often shown expressly to shock audiences.

2. Cartoons are not made just for children.

3. Movies in the 1950s were filmed in color to compete with black-and-white television.

4. Federal laws forbid showing cigarette advertisements on television in the United States.

Activity 10

Drama refers expressly to narrative forms written for performance on the stage by live actors. It has come to refer also to any series of events that involve interesting or conflicting forces.

   Ignoring the politician's speech, the TV camera focused on the drama of the protestors being arrested.

Dramatic or *dramatically* can refer to something that is done in a theatrical or showy manner, or something that is bold or striking in effect.

   One protestor raised his arms dramatically.
   The scene was a dramatic reminder of the political unrest in the country.

Dramatize or dramatization means "to represent something in a bold or striking manner" or "to convey an idea through acting."

The scene dramatized the political unrest.

A dramatization of the scene was included in a recent movie.

Rewrite each of these sentences to include *drama, dramatic, dramatically, dramatize,* or *dramatization.*

1. Live television coverage is able to bring into the home the emotional effect of real events as they are happening.
2. These events are all the more striking because viewers know the events are real and not portrayed by actors.
3. Recently, when a two-year-old child was trapped in an underground well, TV crews rushed to broadcast the daring rescue operations.
4. For seventeen hours the television cameras followed the story of the rescue.
5. The sweat-stained faces of the rescuers boldly showed how hard they were working to dig the little girl out.
6. The most significant moment was when a man emerged from the hole carrying the tiny child in his arms.
7. Knowing the TV cameras were on him, he announced with exaggerated emotion, "She's alive."

Activity 11

Vision (non-count noun) refers to our sense of sight.

As we age, our vision becomes cloudy.

Visions (count noun) refer to mental pictures. *To have visions* means "to have mental pictures, usually of something that is not real." Often these visions reflect a person's fears or secret hopes.

As she began writing her novel, the author had visions of winning the Nobel Prize for literature.

To visualize something can also mean to have a mental picture of something not real, but it more often refers to mental images of things that are real.

As the doctor touched the patient's arm, she visualized the bones and muscles under the skin.

Complete each of these sentences with *visualized* or *had visions of.* Explain your choice.

1. The motion picture director _____ a rainstorm ruining his parade scene.

2. The lighting technician _____ the electrical wiring that would be needed for the lights.

3. The costume designer _____ the leading actress tearing her dress as she danced.

4. The leading actor _____ winning an Academy Award for his performance.

5. The screen storywriter _____ the first scene taking place in a dark, old house.

To envision means ''to imagine'' and can refer to things that are either real or unreal. Substitute *envisioned* in the sentences above.

Activity 12

Visibility refers to the capacity of something to be clearly seen by people.

> *Bicycle riders should wear light-colored clothing at night to increase their visibility. They will be most visible in white. Bicycle riders in dark clothing may be invisible to automobile drivers.*

Restate the following sentences to include *visible*, *invisible*, or *visibility*.

1. The paintings of certain 19th-century artists were so smooth that their brush strokes disappeared.
2. In contrast, Whistler's brush strokes are quite apparent.
3. Obvious brush strokes add texture to a painting.
4. Museums often display a famous painting on a wall by itself so it can be seen better.
5. Only a trained eye can see the differences between an original painting and a clever copy.
6. These differences cannot be seen by the average person.

Activity 13

Visual/visually refer to eyesight. *Visible/visibly* refer to things that are obvious or that can be seen by others. Compare these sentences.

> *The man has a visual handicap.* (The man's eyesight is poor.)
> *The man has a visible handicap.* (The man has a handicap of some sort that is obvious to other people.)

Use *visual/visually* or *visible/visibly* in each sentence. In some sentences, more than one answer is possible.

1. A _____ art is one that can be enjoyed by seeing it, such as painting.

2. The early paintings of Picasso are _____ different from his later works.

3. Someone once said, ''A painting is _____ poetry.''

4. Bright colors are more _____ appealing to young children than muted ones.

5. Visitors to the Sistine Chapel in Rome are _____ impressed by the magnificent ceiling paintings.

> <u>Visual</u> aids are items such as pictures, maps, or charts used in instruction or demonstration.
>
> The teacher used many visual aids to help his students understand current social problems.

Activity 14

Vision (non-count noun) and *visionary* refer to the power of creative thought, especially with regard to the future.

> *Frank Lloyd Wright was a man of vision. His visionary designs helped shape modern architecture.*

In what ways were the following people visionary?

1. Henry Ford
2. Alexander Graham Bell
3. Wilbur and Orville Wright

Activity 15

The words *affect* and *effect* are commonly confused because of their similar spelling and meaning. Although both have a noun form and a verb form, *affect* occurs most frequently in its verb form, and *effect* occurs most frequently in its noun form. *To affect* something or *to have an effect* on something is to is to influence or change something, often in a negative way. The change or influence is not specifically stated.

> *Aging affects our hearing.*
> *Aging has an effect on our hearing.*

When the result or change is specified, a different form is used.

> *One effect of aging is (that) our hearing becomes less sensitive.*

Below are several events that happened after sound was added to films. Make complete sentences by combining one of the phrases below with one of the numbered events. The first two have been done for you.

One effect of adding sound to film was _____
Adding sound to film had an effect on _____
Adding sound to film affected _____

1. movie attendance
> *Adding sound to film had an effect on movie attendance.*
> *Adding sound to film affected movie attendance.*

2. a dramatic increase in movie attendance.
> *One effect of adding sound to film was a dramatic increase in movie attendance.*

3. the careers of actors with poor speaking voices
4. the popularization of musical movies
5. the need to soundproof filming studios
6. the way film stories were narrated
7. the rapid disappearance of silent films
8. theaters had to add sound equipment

Activity 16

One meaning of *popular* is "well-liked by many people." Another meaning is "for the ordinary people."

> *Rogers and Hammerstein wrote popular music. Their musical play* The Sound of Music *was very popular.*

Complete the following sentences, using *popular, popularly, popularize,* or *popularity.*

1. One of the most _____ singers in the _____ music field in the 1950s was Elvis Presley.

2. He introduced a new musical sound that helped _____ rock and roll music.

3. His great _____ was due as much to his new music as to the rhythmic way he moved as he sang.

4. Though _____ with teenagers, he was criticized by adults for his suggestive movements.

5. "Elvis," as he was _____ referred to, played a significant role in the _____ of rock music.

Activity 17

To criticize something or *to be critical* of something means "to find fault" with it. *A critic* is a person who criticizes.

> *Adults are often critical of teenage styles.*
> *Teenagers are criticized for their styles.*

Read the paragraph, then restate the sentences using the word forms given. You may need to add words or change the word order to make the sentences logical.

(**a**) Recently, many old black-and-white films have been colorized to make them more marketable to television stations. (**b**) Many people object to colorization because they say that the black-and-white photography emphasizes the historical nature of the films. (**c**) Also, those who are against colorization say that the colorizing process produces unattractive colors. (**d**) The producers of colorized films have been accused of ruining classics for the sake of making money.

1. (Sentence **b**) critical
2. (Sentence **c**) critics
3. (Sentence **d**) criticized

A person who reviews and comments on new films, stage plays, books, art exhibits, etc., for the media is called a <u>critic</u>.

> Although literary critics praised the author's latest novel, book sales have been poor.

A <u>critique</u> is an evaluation of a literary work or a scholarly article.

> Professors often ask their students to write critiques of articles from periodicals.

Activity 18

Another meaning of *critical* is "essential" or "important."

> *Precise timing is critical when actors perform dangerous movie stunts. Precise timing is critical to the success of the stunts.*

Rewrite each of these sentences to include *critical*. The first one has been done for you.

1. Gathering facts is something a newspaper reporter must do as part of the job.

   Gathering facts is a critical part of a newspaper reporter's job.

2. The reporters' facts must be accurate in their stories.

3. People's names must be spelled correctly.

4. Reporters must be sensitive when reporting tragedies.

5. A newspaper's reputation depends on careful reporting.

> Critical can also mean "serious" or "life-threatening."
> Her condition was critical following the accident.

Activity 19

Literature refers to artistic writings of high quality. Literary, the adjective form, has the added meaning of "well-educated."

> Latin, mathematics, and literature formed the core of university education in past centuries.
>
> Students read the literary works of great thinkers. Upon graduating, they were literary adults.

Literate/literacy refer to the ability to read and write and also refer to having knowledge in certain fields. Illiterate/illiteracy are the negative forms.

> Illiteracy is a major problem in some countries.
> Nowadays, people need to be literate in computers.

Restate the following sentences using literature, literary, literacy, illiteracy, literate, and illiterate.

1. Japan has one of the highest rates in the world of people who can read and write.
2. O. Henry and Oscar Wilde are just two of several authors who wrote books while they were in prison.
3. Statistics show that many criminals are unable to read.
4. Many best-selling books are not well-written works of art.
5. Travel in a foreign country is simplified if you can read the language of the country you are visiting.
6. Some people fear that television will lead to a decrease in reading and writing skills.
7. I am totally ignorant when it comes to science.

Activity 20

Many technical words comprise parts taken from Greek or Latin. For example, the literal, or actual, meaning of thermometer is "heat measure." Thermometer literally means "heat measure."

Match the words on the left with their literal meanings. State the relationships in complete sentences, using literal or literally.

1.	automobile	sound writing
2.	telephone	distant writing
3.	telegraph	distant sound
4.	phonograph	self-moving
5.	autograph	small sound
6.	microphone	self-writing

Activity 21

People often exaggerate when they want to make their statements dramatic, particulary in conversation.

>*My brother eats like a pig.*
>*We were baking from the hot weather.*

To make it clear that they are not exaggerating, speakers may add the word *literally*, which means "in fact."

>*I have literally dozens of cousins.*

Recently, however, people have been using *literally* for emphasis. Probably they mean to use *virtually*.

In small groups, discuss which of these sentences are logically possible and which misuse *literally*.

1. I literally froze to death last night.
2. The freeway traffic literally did not move for an hour.
3. The table was literally covered with ants.
4. She literally has no friends.
5. The house was literally destroyed by the earthquake.
6. I was so hungry that I literally ate everything in sight.
7. I literally cried my eyes out during the movie.
8. He was literally penniless when I met him.

Describe what is happening in the picture. Use *depict*, *expression*, *literally*, *exaggerate*.

USING WORDS IN CONTEXT

Activity 1

The following sentences are in scrambled order. Put them in the correct order by numbering them. When the sentences are read in the correct order, they will result in a coherent narrative.

_____ a. Harry Houdini, one of the most popular magicians of all time, was noted for performing sensational escapes.

_____ b. As hundreds of people watched from the nearby shores, four assistants dramatically tied Houdini's hands and feet.

_____ c. Therefore, whenever he created a new escape act, he expressly dramatized its danger.

_____ d. To enhance the visual drama, they covered his eyes with a blindfold.

_____ e. He was not only an escape artist; he was also a showman with a superior sense of drama.

_____ f. For example, one of his escape acts began on a bridge 100 feet above a rushing river.

_____ g. Then the assistants lifted Houdini into a large metal box, closed the water-tight lid and with exaggerated effort, tossed the box into the river.

_____ h. For ten long minutes the onlookers focused their attention on the water.

_____ i. Suddenly an arm was visible, then a face.

_____ j. Others prayed quietly and were visibly upset.

_____ k. But soon they began to express concern, and some criticized Houdini for staging such a dangerous stunt.

_____ l. As the minutes passed, they envisioned Houdini near death in his underwater box.

_____ m. At first the mood of the onlookers was confident.

_____ n. Houdini was alive! What a sensational escape!

Activity 2

Read the following paragraph as many times as you can in three mintues. Then close the book and rewrite as much of the information as you can.

Compact discs, or CDs as they are popularly called, have revolutionized the recorded music industry. When CDs were introduced in 1983, no one envisioned the sensational rise in popularity that this new recorded music medium would experience. In just five years, CD sales comprised over 50 percent of recorded music sales in some stores and became the most popular medium of recorded music, followed by cassette tapes. Simultaneously, long-playing record albums experienced a dramatic drop in sales after dominating the market for forty years. In some areas, long-playing albums have literally disappeared from music stores and compact discs have taken their place.

Activity 3

Your instructor will dictate a paragraph about a 1938 radio program called "War of the Worlds" that created widespread panic. After you have written the paragraph, work with a partner to fill in words you may have missed or to correct grammar and spelling. When you and your partner believe that your paragraphs are correct, compare your versions to the paragraph printed at the back of the book. Make necessary corrections.

Topics for Writing or Discussion

1. Find a human interest story in a newspaper. Discuss how this story could be depicted as a television drama. What scenes would you create? What narrative function would each scene serve?

2. Compare news reporting on television and news reporting in newspapers. What are the advantages and disadvantages of each?

3. Imagine that you are a film critic. Discuss a recent film you have seen, describing both its good and bad features.

4. Find a political cartoon in a newspaper or magazine. What does the cartoon depict? What message does it convey?

5. In many ways, writing a composition is like creating a motion picture. What similarities can you identify?

6
NOURISHING NATIONS: PAST AND PRESENT

ESTABLISHING A CONTEXT

Pre-reading Discussion

- Name a food that you have recently eaten. Trace it from your table back to its source.
- Why do people from different cultures prefer different foods? What factors influence these preferences?
- Can you name any inventions that are related to the collecting, storing, transporting, or preparing of food?

> Read this article for general meaning. If you cannot understand the meaning of the content, use a dictionary to look up key words (words that are important to the meaning).

(1) Human history has been shaped by a preoccupation with food. Ever since prehistoric times, the search for food has determined where people have lived, what they have invented, who they have befriended, and how they have lived. Throughout history, conditions related to the food supply have determined where ports and cities were built, where expeditions of exploration were sent, which wars were fought, and who would rule nations. Nothing has occupied more human time and energy than the tasks related to finding, collecting, transporting, and preparing food. Food both reflects the societies in which it is found and shapes the character of the people in them. As a famous food historian said in the 19th century, "The destiny of nations has depended on how they have nourished themselves."

(2) From their earliest moments on earth, people have been preoccupied with food. Prehistoric humans were first hunters of animals and gatherers of plants. Some of the earliest human inventions were related to the human pursuit and preparation of food. Spears and clubs, for example, were created for the purpose of hunting. A particularly significant innovation, the ability to control and use fire, changed life considerably and prepared the way for an entirely new diet. Using fire in cooking made edible

some formerly indigestible foods and probably greatly improved human health, since heat helps to break down the food fibers and release protein and carbohydrates. The controlling of fire therefore led humankind to a longer life-span and stronger existence.

(3)   Prehistoric life was nomadic. Not until people began to cultivate their own food and raise animals did they see the need to settle in one place. They then formed permanent communities where they could await the cycles of the seasons and combine their efforts to farm the land. This led to more time for leisure and for the development of better agricultural tools and techniques. Such innovations as pottery, the calendar, and water management resulted from the needs of these early farmers. Thus, food influenced the most fundamental of choices, including where people lived, how they regulated their environment, and how they expressed their creativity.

(4)   The food preferences of a civilization both reflect its environment and determine its habits. The civilizations that lived in rich pasturelands, such as those in the Middle East, developed the capability of domesticating sheep, goats, and cattle. As a result, meat was an important part of their diet. On the other hand, the people of other cultures, such as those in South America and Asia, raised almost no animals and consumed almost no meat because they lived on land that could not support large herds. Partly because of their vegetarian diet, the Asians often had trouble stopping the aggressions of their meat-eating enemies, who tended to be stronger. From these vegetarian civilizations we have inherited a tremendous variety of domesticated plants such as corn, potatoes, beans, gourds, squash, tomatoes, peanuts, green peppers, cocoa beans, vanilla beans, peas, cucumbers, wheat, barley, and rice.

(5)   In some cases, the history of an individual food reveals insights into cultural preferences and cross-cultural relationships. The potato, for example, is usually attributed to the Irish but was actually used widely by the Inca Indians in Peru as early as A.D. 100. After Pizarro's conquest of the Incas in 1537, the potato was taken back to Spain. Although the Spanish refused to eat it, they raised it to feed to their animals. Spanish settlers later took it to eat on the long voyage to Florida in 1560 because it didn't spoil easily. After the British raided the Spanish in Florida, the potato was among the "valuables" that they took back to England, but the British wouldn't eat it either. But when the potato was introduced in Ireland, it was immediately adopted as the national food. Today the potato is widely popular in Europe. In fact, nine times more potatoes are produced in Europe than in the United States. The potato has become a part of the everyday diet in many Western cultures.

(6)   The transformation from eating for survival to dining for pleasure took place in ancient Greece and Rome where the upper class cultivated the art of dining and gave food new prestige. During the Roman Empire, feasts commonly lasted for days, and hosts tried to impress their guests with spectacular banquets that might include such extravagances as field mice, nightingale tongues, ostrich brains, parrot heads, camel heels, elephant trunks, and carp that had been fattened on a diet of human slave meat. Gluttony and wastefulness were so excessive that laws were passed at various times to enforce moderation by legislating the cost of a meal, the number of guests, or the variety of dishes, but these laws were consistently ignored by the aristocracy. Just as Rome

Like farmers throughout the world, this Bolivian farmer devotes most of his time and energy to the pursuit of food. Photo by James Sawders.

lived by its appetite, it may have died by it as well. Some historians speculate that one of the causes of the fall of the Roman Empire was lead poisoning. The water supply may have been contaminated with lead because of the use of leaden irrigation pipes. In addition, the Roman aristocracy may have died off as a result of using leaden cooking vessels to cook wine-based syrups and sauces. These foods absorbed an especially heavy dose of lead, which is fatal in large quantities. The poor, who used ordinary earthenware cooking pots, avoided this chemical reaction.

(7)   It has been said that food was partially responsible for both the rise and the fall of the Roman Empire. Soon after Rome fell, social order virtually vanished and civilization halted. Bridges collapsed, roads fell into disrepair, communication stopped, and communities eventually became isolated. As a result of this isolation, the importing and exporting of food stopped and a fight for survival began. The sophisticated agricultural techniques and the art of selective breeding of animals were soon forgotten. Fields were allowed to become overgrown, and animals were undernourished.

When there was a shortage of meat, people slaughtered their plow animals. This left them with no animals to plow their fields and led to subsequent food shortages. During this period, known as the Dark Ages, food again became a necessity instead of a pleasure. The only visible attention to food at this time was given by Catholic holy men, known as monks. Although they led a simple life, they kept alive the tradition of "dining" through their pleasure of good food. The religious ideal of hard work motivated them to produce food for the surrounding areas, and their communities eventually developed into resourceful industries that helped Europe acquire productive skills again.

(8)   By early in the 15th century, Europe had recovered its appetite for fine food and was sending explorers around the world for exotic foods and spices. This led to the discovery of the Americas and to the first European settlements in North America. The first American settlers at Jamestown were mostly refined "gentlemen" who had never done any physical work and had no interest in doing so. The winter of 1609–1610 became known as the "Starving Time," because four out of five people starved. If the Native American Indians hadn't helped the settlers, they all would have died. Food thus became the basis for the first relationships between the settlers and the Native Americans. Indian influence on the developing dietary habits of the American settlers cannot be overstated: 80 percent of the present American food plants were unknown to Europeans before Columbus's arrival in North America in 1492.

(9)   Just as in many other wars throughout history, food was very influential in the starting of the American Revolution. The British taxes on imported tea and molasses made the early American patriots angry enough to fight. John Adams called molasses "an essential ingredient to American Independence." In addition, the knowledge that the patriots could survive without imported food surely helped give them the confidence to fight for independence.

(10)   The influence of food on the United States did not stop with the American Revolution. Many of the immigrants who have flocked to the United States throughout history have come because of the rich food supply. For example, thousands of Irish immigrated to the United States in 1846 because of Ireland's potato famine. In addition to influencing immigrants to move to the United States, food influenced how they survived and prospered once they arrived. Many of the inventions that made people affluent and have determined the direction of American industry were related to agriculture and food production. These included the McCormick reaper in 1834, the ice-making machine in 1830, and the machine-made can in 1868.

(11)   People today are no less influenced by food than were their predecessors. Americans annually spend an estimated $250 billion on food. About 10 percent of that is spent on fast food, and another large portion in other restaurants. In fact, since 1980, Americans have eaten less than half of their meals at home. An abundance of other trends have affected both American eating habits and food-related industries, including processed foods, microwavable foods, "natural" foods, gourmet foods, and diet foods, which alone capture 30 percent of the American food budget. Although the quality of American food may have decreased as a result of mass production and high technology, its prominence in daily life was never more visible.

(12)   The role of food in the future is certain to be no less decisive than it has been in the past. The need for human ingenuity has never been more apparent than it is now as various parts of the world face inequitable food supplies and the loss of natural resources from misuse and overuse. Also apparent is the need for governmental attention to issues related to world hunger and environmental effects on the food chain. It is certain that as the future direction of the world unfolds, food will continue to play an essential role.

Comprehension Check

The purpose of this activity is to check your understanding of the article and to give practice using vocabulary words. Label each sentence true or false according to the article. If you cannot understand the meaning of a sentence, use a dictionary to look up key words.

1. The earliest humans were vegetarian nomads.
2. When people began cooking their food, some formerly digestible foods became indigestible.
3. Initially, sheep, goats, and cattle were domesticated in the Middle East.
4. Because of their diet, the early Asians were the aggressors against their meat-eating enemies.
5. The Spanish and the British cultivated potatoes, but they didn't regard them as food for people.
6. Field mice and parrot heads formed a fundamental part of the diet of the early Incas.
7. During the Roman Empire, the aristocracy helped enforce laws that required moderation.
8. The monks taught people to be resourceful during the unproductive Dark Ages.
9. The first American settlers almost died in Jamestown because of the aggressions of the Indians.
10. The world's natural resources are distributed equitably around the globe.

UNDERSTANDING WORDS

Vocabulary List

Verbs	Nouns	Adjectives/ Participles	Adverbials
absorb	aggression	dietary	formerly
attribute	destiny	(in)equitable	throughout
consume	dining	excessive	
contaminate	existence	fundamental	
cultivate	ingenuity	indigestible	
enforce	moderation	processed	
isolate	preoccupation	resourceful	
nourish	prominence	selective	
produce	pursuit	undernourished	
survive			

Subject-Specific Vocabulary

Verbs: domesticate, starve. **Nouns:** agriculture, carbohydrate, diet, fibers,
Adjectives: edible, vegetarian. protein.

Activity 1

Cross out the word or phrase that does not have the same meaning as the others.

1. In prehistoric times, people (survived/existed/progressed/continued living) by hunting and gathering food.

2. The (pursuit/hunt/chase/crusade) for food led to the invention of weapons for hunting.

3. The cooking of raw foods resulted in dietary improvements and provided a stronger (potential/life/existence) for humans.

4. Food had an influence on the (fundamental/primary/basic/accessible) choice of where people lived.

5. When humans (tamed/raised/domesticated/expanded) animals, meat became a basic part of their diet.

6. The potato has been (credited to/traced to/based on/attributed to) the Irish.

7. People (consumed/ate/cultivated/devoured) a/an (unique/overabundant/excessive/unreasonable) amount of food at Roman banquets.

8. The (existence/dominance/prominence/significance) of food in everyday life in America is visible in the home, in food markets, in restaurants, and in food-related industries.

9. The food supply in various parts of the world is (uneven/dissimilar/unpredictable/inequitable).

10. After the fall of the Roman Empire, the Catholic monks developed (innovative/resourceful/inventive/new) industries to help revive productive skills in Europe.

Activity 2

Describe the relationship between the following words (antonyms, synonyms, neither):

1. cultivate/produce
2. nourish/starve
3. destiny/fate
4. existence/purpose
5. survive/die
6. fundamental/practical
7. inequitable/unfair
8. existence/life
9. innovation/ingenuity
10. formerly/previously

Activity 3

Circle the appropriate word for each of the following sentences. The words are not synonyms, but in some sentences, both words make logical sentences with different meanings. If both words are suitable, circle them both. Be prepared to explain your answers.

1. Contaminated food (nourishes/harms) people.
2. A person can (die/survive) in an excessively cold climate.
3. The collection of homemade gadgets in my mother's kitchen shows how (resourceful/impractical) she is.
4. Traffic laws are (enforced/determined) by the police.
5. Human (uniformity/ingenuity) is important for problem-solving.
6. A healthy diet includes (excessive/moderate) amounts of sugar.
7. Agricultural experts (attribute/enforce) the failure of certain crops to the pollution in the environment.
8. The dog was first (cultivated/domesticated) in prehistoric times.
9. Food was considered to be the greatest source of pleasure (after/throughout) the Roman Empire.
10. In light of the child's contagious disease, his mother decided to (separate/isolate) him from his siblings.

Activity 4

Substitute a synonym from the vocabulary list for each word or group of words in parentheses. Be sure to keep the original meaning of the sentence.

1. Excessive amounts of minerals will (poison) the water supply.
2. Dieticians suggest that alcoholic beverages are not harmful if consumed in (small or reasonable amounts).
3. When people are overweight, they must be (particular) about their dietary choices.
4. Food is one of the most (basic) of human needs.
5. From time to time, we enjoy (eating) at fashionable restaurants.
6. The desire for exotic foods and spices led to the European (search) for new lands.

7. The actress was inundated with attention because of her (fame).

8. Getting an education is a worthwhile (venture).

9. The man was preoccupied with a desire to foresee his (future).

10. Unlike meat-eaters, vegetarians (maintain) themselves primarily on vegetables and fruits.

Activity 5

The word *absorb* means "to take in."

> They absorbed the good news about their lost daughter with great relief.

It can also mean "to accept responsibility for."

> She absorbed the cost of repairing the car.

Another meaning is "to suck up in the manner of a sponge."

> The dry land quickly absorbed the rain.

When used in reference to a person, this word has the more figurative meaning of "to engross completely or occupy wholly."

> He was absorbed by the book for hours.

Name something or someone that absorbs each of the following items:

heat	water	the cost of a wedding
a child's attention	your attention	the blame for unpopular laws

Activity 6

During the Roman Empire, the eating habits of the upper class were extravagant and their appetites excessive. Circle any of the following words that could be used to further identify their diets. Explain.

moderate	inventive	vegetarian	selective
resourceful	frugal	unique	equitable

Activity 7

Eating was transformed to dining during the Roman Empire. That is, people ate for pleasure rather than merely to satisfy hunger. Which of the following conditions probably existed during the Roman Empire?

1. Parents tried to help their children cultivate good table manners.

2. The consumption of alcohol increased.

3. Food preparation required an excessive amount of time.

4. A chef who cooked with ingenuity was not valued greatly.

5. People were less selective about the quality of their food than former civilizations had been.

Activity 8

Resourcefulness is the ability to find a way around difficulties, and it is used only in reference to people.

> *The resourceful secretary used paper clips to fix the broken typewriter.*
> *The children survived the famine because of the resourcefulness of their mother in finding food.*

Ed Simpson was lost in the desert alone, and the only things he had with him were the items listed below on the left. Since he was a very resourceful person, he was able to accomplish each of the tasks on the right. Match the items that you think he used with each of the tasks, showing how he demonstrated his resourcefulness.

Resources	**Tasks**
a raincoat	He signaled for help in the daytime.
mirror	He gathered water from the dew.
a flashlight	He sheltered himself from the sun.
	He built a fire.
	He dug for buried roots for food.

A <u>resource</u> is something that is used for aid or support. Natural <u>resources</u> refer to products or advantages that are supplied by nature.

> Most of the country's natural resources were affected by the disastrous flood.

People <u>pool their resources</u> when they combine their resources for one mutual purpose.

> The children pooled their resources so they could buy a nice gift for the teacher.

Activity 9

The word *consume* has several meanings. It can mean "to eat or drink."

> *The students consumed excessive amounts of beer.*

It can also mean "to engross or absorb completely."

> *The book consumed my attention.*

It can also mean "to use up or destroy."

> *Enormous quantities of gasoline are consumed by American automobiles.*

Under what circumstances and by whom would each of the following be consumed?

3 glasses of water	oil	a newspaper story
5 gallons of beer	2 hamburgers	a book
a ton of fish	a love letter	technological information
a tree		a town

Activity 10

Ingenuity refers to the process of being clever or inventive, or having an original idea. It is only used in reference to humans or to humanlike intelligence.

> *The ingenuity of Robert Noyce led to the development of the integrated circuit and the microprocessor.*

What resulted from the ingenuity of each of the following people?
Stephen Wozniak and Steven Jobs
Thomas Edison
the first humans

Activity 11

Which of the following occurrences are a result of human ingenuity? Explain.

the end of World War II	acid rain	the Julian calendar
the personal computer	heavy traffic	the vernal equinox
the world's inequitable food supply	earthquakes	overpopulation

Activity 12

Throughout is usually used as a preposition. It means "from beginning to end" in reference to time or "everywhere" in reference to space (place).

> *We thought about your question throughout the evening.*
> *Potatoes were used as animal feed throughout Europe.*

Replace each of the underlined phrases with a phrase beginning with *throughout.* The first one is done for you.

1. After eating lunch together, the two students studied <u>from 1:00 to 4:00</u>. *(throughout the afternoon)*
2. Rice is a fundamental part of the diet <u>in every Asian country</u>.
3. <u>From early 1600 until early 1700</u>, Americans were attempting to decrease their dependence on imported food products.
4. After the power went off, the clocks were unsynchronized <u>in every classroom</u>.

Activity 13

In pairs or small groups, discuss the following questions.

1. Before people cooked their food, many meats and plants were inedible. Which of the following foods would be inedible if you did not cook them? (Answers may vary).

beef	nuts	lettuce	rice
carrots	corn	oysters	cabbage
beans	tomatoes	fish	potatoes
popcorn			

What are some other examples of foods that are inedible when raw?
What are some examples of foods that are indigestible when raw?

2. Which inventions have helped decrease food contamination? Explain.

3. What are the most fundamental human needs? What are the most fundamental human rights?

4. What do you know about the dietary habits in other countries? What do the people eat and drink? What do they avoid?

5. Tell who might wish to pursue each of the following:

a speeding car	a boyfriend	a hobby
an education	a college degree	happiness

PUTTING WORDS INTO SENTENCES

Ten words have been selected from the original vocabulary list for closer study. These words and their related forms are listed below.

Verbs	Nouns	Adjectives/Participles	Adverbials
absorb	absorption	(un)absorbed	
		(un)absorbing	
		absorbent	
attribute (to)	attribute	attributed	
consume	consumer	consumed	
	consumption	consuming	
cultivate	cultivation	cultivated	
exceed	excess	(un)excessive	excessively
exist	existence	existent	
	nonexistence	nonexistent	
produce	production	(un)productive	(un)productively
	producer		
pursue	pursuit	pursued	
		pursuing	

Verbs	Nouns	Adjectives/ Participles	Adverbials
	resource	(un)resourceful	resourcefully
	resourcefulness		
survive	survival	surviving	
	survivor		

Activity 1

The word *cultivate* refers to the process of preparing the land for a crop and encouraging its growth.

They cultivated the vegetables.

The pictures on page 133 show a progression of events that occur between the time tomatoes are planted and the time they are eaten as catsup. Use as many of the given words as possible to write sentences describing the illustrated sequence of events.

cultivate	cultivation	cultivated	consumer
consume	consumption	produce	production
producer	productively	productive	

Activity 2

Use the information in Table 6.1 to write sentences about the production of rice in the world. Use the provided words in the order they are given.

Table 6.1   The Leading Countries in Rice Production, 1985

China	X X X X X X X X X X X
India	X X X X /
Indonesia	X X /
Bangladesh	X /
Thailand	X /
Vietnam	X 1/4
Japan	X

X = 15,000,000 metric tons
Source: Dept of Agriculture, *World Book*, 1988.

---

1. the Chinese/producers
2. produced/Vietnam/in 1985
3. Indonesians/produced/in 1985
4. production/exceeds
5. produced/more than
6. less than/produced

Activity 3

A recent study at a university in British Columbia tested the Vitamin C absorption of five healthy young men. The study lasted 4 weeks. Use the information in the following chart to discover the results, and then answer the following questions. Use the words in parentheses in your answer.

Table 6.2   Absorption Rate of Vitamin C

Dosage in mg/day	Weeks			
	1	2	3	4
6000				D
5000				
4000				
3000			D	
2000		D		
1500			A	A
1000	D	A		
500	A			

D = dosage of Vitamin C
A = absorption of Vitamin C

1. How much Vitamin C was assimilated after one week? (absorbed)
2. When was the greatest amount of Vitamin C absorbed? (absorption)
3. Does the rate of absorption of Vitamin C increase at the same pace as the rate of consumption? (absorbed)
4. Does the body assimilate more Vitamin C when larger amounts are consumed? (absorption)

Activity 4

Use the information in Figure 6.1 to describe the amount of consumption of sugar between 1909 and 1971. Use the words indicated.

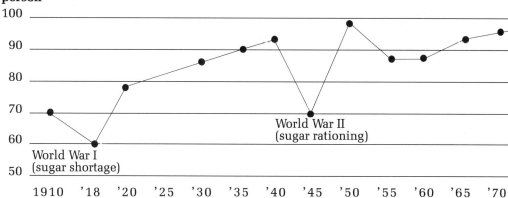

Figure 6.1 U.S. Sugar Consumption

Pounds of sugar per person

World War II
(sugar rationing)

World War I
(sugar shortage)

Source: U.S. Department of Agriculture

1. consumed/1910
2. consumption/1930/exceeded
3. consumers/after World War II
4. continued to consume/in 1965

5. an increase in sugar consumption/ after World War I
6. consumption/decreased dramatically
7. consuming/since 1950

Activity 5

Reread paragraph four of the article in this chapter before beginning to answer the following questions. Your answers should be complete sentences that use the words in parentheses.

1. Did the Asians believe that meat was necessary for their survival? (survive)
2. Why were the Asian people often unsuccessful in their battles against the people of the Middle East? (consumption)
3. Describe the Asian diet. (consumed)
4. What foods did the Asian people depend upon to survive? (survival)
5. What foods did the Middle Eastern people depend upon for survival? (survived on)
6. Name three foods that have survived since the early vegetarian civilizations of the Incas. (surviving) (adj)

Activity 6

To exist can mean "to live or be real" and is often used with the same meaning as the structures *there is* or *there are*.

> *Crime exists in our society.*
> *There is a lot of crime in our society.*
> *Dinosaurs no longer exist.*
> *There are no dinosaurs in the modern world.*

Rewrite each of the following sentences, substituting the appropriate tenses of *exist* for *there is/are* and likewise substituting *there is/are* for *exist*. You may add or delete information as needed, but do not alter the meaning.

1. Sophisticated methods of irrigation existed in the Assyrian and Babylonian societies as early as 800 B.C.
2. There are 18 words in the Provencal language for *bread*, depending on how it is cooked.
3. Hostilities have often existed between vegetarian and meat-eating cultures.
4. In the Mediterranean countries, hundreds of proverbs about the word *bread* exist.
5. Political strife often exists in a nation where people lack food.

Activity 7

The words *nonexistent* and *nonexistence* can be used to refer to the absence of existence.

> *Regulations on food purity were nonexistent before 1860.*
> *The nonexistence of regulations on food purity resulted in many deaths.*

Following is a list of inventions and a description of a problem that continued as long as the invention was nonexistent. For each item in this list, write sentences that use the words in parentheses. You may need to combine the given information by using a word like *because*, *when*, or *after*. The first one is done for you.

Problems   **Inventions**
1. Cooking on a wood stove was difficult.   The gas stove was invented in 1880.
   (nonexistent, nonexistence)

   a. *The gas stove was nonexistent before 1880.* OR *When the gas stove was nonexistent, cooking was difficult.*
   b. *Because of the nonexistence of the gas stove, cooking was difficult.*

2. Meat could not be transported. (non-   The ice-making machine was
   existent, nonexistence)   invented in 1830.
3. Food was expensive to preserve. (non-   Machine-made cans were invented
   existent, existence)   in 1868.

4. Sugarcane was the only source of sugar and was expensive. (existent, existence)

Sugar beets were developed in 1801.

> **To coexist** means to exist together, in or at the same place or time.
> The Indians and the early Americans coexisted in relative peace.

Activity 8

The words *exist* and *survive* are sometimes interchangeable because they both refer to the continuance of being or of life. *Survival*, however, means "to live or exist beyond another event," and that event is often implied or referred to in the sentence. *Survival*, therefore, can be defined as "to remain in existence."

Restate the following sentences, using the words in parentheses.

1. The water supply in Rome was contaminated with lead. (existed)
2. The early American settlers were able to endure the first miserable winters because the Indians taught them to cultivate native foods. (survived)
3. The early American settlers' diet consisted of nuts and berries. (existed on)
4. Because of the monks, the love for good food continued to exist after the Dark Ages. (survived)

Activity 9

To attribute is often used to credit a source of information or of origin.

> *We attribute this saying to Shakespeare.*
> *The computer wizard attributed his success to hard work.*
> *Leap year is attributed to the fact that an extra day accumulates over time.*

Match one item in Column 1 with one item each in Columns 2 and 3 to form grammatical and logical sentences. Write three sentences using *attribute to* and write three sentences using *is attributed to*. Add other words as necessary.

Column 1	Column 2	Column 3
people	popularization of potato	American Indians
scientists	transformation of "eating" to "dining"	the Romans
historians		Inca Indians
geographers	emigration of Irish	the Irish
psychologists	domestication of cocoa beans	potato blight
	survival of first American settlers	environment
	personality differences between twins	

Activity 10

Read the paragraph, then restate the sentences using the word forms below. You may need to add words or change the word order to make the sentences logical.

(a) UNICEF (The United Nations International Children's Emergency Fund) is an international organization that has been fighting to help protect the world's under-priviledged children since 1946. (b) UNICEF believes that many of the world's children who die because of disease could remain alive if better sanitation were practiced. (c) It is estimated that 50 percent of the diseased children who die every day should not have to die. (d) As it is, the children who don't die live an existence of poverty.

1. (Sentence a) (for the) survival
2. (Sentence b) survive
3. (Sentence c) survive
4. (Sentence d) barely able to survive

Activity 11

To pursue/in pursuit of something refer to seeking after something or following something with the intent of capturing or achieving it.

He is pursuing a high school diploma.
Two police cars were in pursuit of the robber.

Read the paragraph, then restate the numbered sentences, using the word forms below. You may need to add words or change the word order to make the sentences logical.

(a) What should people eat when they are in pursuit of perfect health? (b) Millions of Americans turn to health food stores when they are pursuing a healthful diet. (c) Food bought in a health food store is more expensive than its counterpart in a grocery store, but many people ignore cost when they are searching for good health. (d) They believe that the pursuit of good health will lead them to a better appearance and a longer life, so they disregard the cost.

1. (Sentence a) pursuing
2. (Sentence b) in pursuit of
3. (Sentence c) when people pursue
4. (Sentence d) pursue

USING WORDS IN CONTEXT

Activity 1

Your instructor will dictate a paragraph about junk food. After you have written the paragraph, work with a partner to fill in words you may have missed or to correct grammar and spelling. When you and your partner believe your paragraphs are correct, compare them to the paragraph printed at the back of the book. Make any necessary corrections.

Activity 2

The following sentences are in scrambled order. Indicate their correct order by numbering them. When the sentences are read in the correct order, they will result in a coherent paragraph. The first one is done for you.

_____ a. The drive-in appealed to this love for the car because people could have a relaxing meal without leaving their cars; they would park their cars in the drive-in spaces, and the waitresses would come to serve them.

_____ b. They were thereby able to serve good food at moderate prices to a public who had formerly eaten nearly all their meals at home.

_____ c. Whereas the diner had appealed to a public absorbed with train travel, the drive-in appealed to people who loved the car.

_____ d. Like the railroad cars, they were built out of mass-produced materials and were the ultimate in efficiency and modern technology.

_____ e. When the pace of life became faster, even the drive-in restaurant wasn't fast enough for the American life style.

_____ f. The diners remained popular throughout the 1950s until they were replaced by another innovation, the drive-in restaurant.

_____ g. The ingenuity of the designers led them to build the diners to resemble railroad cars at a time when train travel was very popular; the public associated them with the speed, mobility, and efficiency of the railroad.

_____ h. This allowed the customer to eat a meal while continuing to drive.

_____ i. The first fast-food restaurant was the roadside diner, which was introduced late in the 19th century.

_____ j. The drive-ins were eventually replaced by drive-through restaurants that offered food that could be taken out of the restaurant and eaten in the car.

__1__ k. Fast food is a prominent part of American life because it is convenient and it fits into the modern life style.

Activity 3

Name a food that you have recently eaten. Draw a diagram that traces it from its source to your table, and label the steps in its progression. The following words and their forms may be useful: cultivate, produce, dietary, processed, throughout, formerly, edible, consume, nourish, attribute, existence.

Activity 4

Read the following paragraph as many times as you can in three minutes. Then with your book closed, rewrite as much of the information as you can remember.

There are many reasons why people are obese, or seriously overweight. The causes include heredity, lack of exercise, personality, and poor dietary habits. Scientists attribute some people's obesity to the number and size of their fat cells. Fat cells are fundamental components of human fat, and scientists are able to count them and measure their size. Some people are fat because they have an excessive number of fat cells, and others are fat because their fat cells are excessively large, that is overfilled with fat. Once a fat cell is formed, it does not disappear; a fat cell can survive the most extreme diet. If weight is lost, a fat cell will get smaller, but it will always be waiting to grow again to its former size.

Topics for Writing or Discussion

1. Imagine that you are a doctor and you have been asked to write an article for a newspaper suggesting ways to lose weight. Write an article that is both informative and convincing.

2. Describe someone you know who has very selective eating habits (a child, an elderly person, a person who is living in an unfamiliar culture, a teenager, a wealthy person, a vegetarian, etc.). Describe this person's diet, and if possible, explain why s/he makes these choices.

3. What three foods do you think are the most commonly eaten throughout the world? Why?

4. Compare and contrast the attitudes toward food during the Roman Empire to those in the modern United States.

Many of the immigrants who have flocked to the United States, like this family at Ellis Island in 1905, have come because of the rich food supply. Photo by Lewis Hine, courtesy of the Library of Congress.

7

ENABLING THE DISABLED

ESTABLISHING A CONTEXT

Pre-reading Discussion

- What architectural barriers are faced by people in wheelchairs? (Consider the home, the workplace, and the community.)
- In what ways would your life be different if you were blind?
- In what ways would your life be different if you were deaf?
- What accommodations have been made by businesses and government services to allow for the needs of people who are disabled?

> Read this article for general meaning. If you cannot understand the meaning of the content, use a dictionary to look up key words (words that are important to the meaning).

(1)   After David Pollard turned off his alarm clock at 6:00 A.M., he got out of bed so he would have time to eat breakfast before driving to work. His morning routine was like that of millions of other people, except for one major difference: David Pollard is quadriplegic; that is, he is unable to move his arms or his legs. He turned off his alarm clock by using a special computer that he controlled by moving his eyebrow. The same computer allowed him to control the lights and adjust the radio. Although he needed help getting out of bed, he moved himself about his apartment in an electric wheelchair, and started his coffee maker by using a voice-activated device. He drove himself to work in a specially equipped van that he was able to enter and operate by using adaptive devices that he controlled with his breath. Although David's life is not easy and nothing can replace the physical abilities that he lost in a car accident, he is determined to live an active and productive life. Modern technology and human inventiveness have given him opportunities that were unforeseen only a few short years ago.

(2)   David Pollard's disability resulted from spinal cord injuries suffered in a car accident. More than 8,500 people each year experience spinal cord injuries, and thousands of others become disabled as a result of accidents or disease. Others are born

with birth defects. Each disability is unique. For example, the results of a spinal cord injury depend on where the spinal cord is injured. One victim of a spinal cord injury may be left a paraplegic, that is, paralyzed below the waist, while another victim may be paralyzed below the chin. Modern medicine is making it increasingly possible to prolong the lives of seriously injured people, so we are seeing increased numbers of people living with severe physical disabilities.

(3)   Until recently it was unusual to see severely handicapped people in public. They couldn't get into or out of most buildings. They couldn't ride subways, buses, or planes, and they couldn't use public telephones or public restrooms. The blind, the deaf, and the immobile were not allowed to attend most public schools, and they found it difficult or impossible to get jobs. In addition, many able-bodied people were insensitive to them, and the handicapped were often the objects of discrimination. In the 1960s, after black civil rights groups had begun fighting racial discrimination, disabled people began to organize themselves and to expose the fact that they, too, were being denied their basic human and legal rights.

(4)   Legal victories for the disabled began to occur in the 1970s, first with the passage of laws guaranteeing that the disabled could not be excluded from public services or public jobs on the basis of their handicaps. Government institutions, schools, cities, and a myriad of other organizations were thereby required to change their architecture and their attitudes to allow access to handicapped people. For example, public parking lots were required to designate a certain number of parking spaces for the exclusive use of disabled people. Such actions had a large impact on Americans and vividly emphasized the fact that disabled people deserved and intended to be a vocal and visible part of public life.

(5)   Many architectural changes were made in public places to accommodate the simple yet critical requirements of the disabled. Doors and aisles were widened and ramps were built for people in wheelchairs. Few buildings were exempt; even the Lincoln Memorial in Washington, D.C., was outfitted with both an elevator and a ramp, as were numerous other places of national interest. Only after the public was exposed to the needs of the handicapped did people begin to realize the tremendous scope of the changes that would have to be made to accommodate these needs. In May 1977, for example, the White House planned a Conference on the Handicapped at Washington's Sheraton-Park Hotel. In order to accommodate disabled delegates, the hotel ordered thousands of dollars' worth of permanent renovations. Bathroom doors had to be replaced, and sinks and public telephones had to be lowered for people in wheelchairs. Menus had to be written in Braille, and the printed letters on signs had to be raised for the blind. Spoken announcements had to be supplemented with lights or printed instructions for the deaf. Since that time, such changes have become commonplace, but the able-bodied public is still surprised by and often insensitive to the special needs of the disabled.

(6)   Other accommodations for the disabled have been introduced by companies wishing to appeal to the needs of their handicapped customers. Certain investment firms have installed teletypewriters in their offices whereby deaf investors can see investment information on a screen and type in their responses on a computer terminal.

It has become commonplace to see wheelchair athletes, such as these in New York City, participate in marathons and other athletic events. Photo by Marc P. Anderson.

An Arizona department store has hired salespeople who are proficient in sign language so they can serve deaf customers. Several major cities publish telephone directories that include listings of buildings and businesses that are wheelchair accessible. National fashion magazines have published articles about practical and fashionable clothing for women in wheelchairs (''Avoid back seams, pockets, and zippers,'' for example). Shopping for the disabled is made simpler by a specialized home computer that describes local products and prices, and then enables the customer to make the purchase from home.

(7)   Similarly, tremendous changes have been seen in the workplace, allowing even severely disabled people the independence that results from having their own jobs. AT&T, for example, employs blind telephone operators who use Braille and audible messages to keep track of information that sighted operators monitor by sight. A quadriplegic employee can ''type'' by using a light pen that is attached to the head. When the pen is focused on the image of a letter, that letter is recorded as ''typed'' by the minicomputer. This ''typewriter'' also serves as the only form of communication for

quadriplegics who have no voices. It is also possible to purchase a breath-activated typewriter or a communications system that allows a person to "draw" an image on a video monitor by eye movement alone.

(8)   Technological innovations also give homebound disabled people the chance to acquire jobs. One wheelchair-bound woman who couldn't handle the rigors of traveling to an office every day found a research and consulting firm that allows her to work at home. She receives her work assignments each morning through telecommunication, that is, electronically through the use of a computer and the telephone. She uses her home computer to complete her assigned tasks, which include database management, wordprocessing, mailings, research, and editing the company newsletter. Similar equipment that allows a worker to be in direct communication with the office while remaining at home is used by many disabled workers who want to be self-sufficient. The training is short-term, and the cost of the equipment is decreasing every year.

(9)   Perhaps the needs of the disabled are most apparent in the home. The simple tasks of controlling one's own environment can be exhausting or even impossible for a disabled person. Computerized units have been designed to accomplish a myriad of these tasks: to raise and lower the lights at prearranged times, to answer the telephone, to control the heat, to start the coffee maker in the morning, to turn locks off and on, and so on. Some of these units are controlled automatically, while others are activated in one of three ways: by an easily operated switch attached to the person's wheelchair, by the person's voice, or by the person's breath. Some units feature fire-alerting functions that are activated by a smoke alarm or by a heat-sensing device. When signaled, the device calls the fire department and other prearranged numbers for help. For those disabled people who prefer not to be so dependent on high technology, other assistive methods are available. Dogs are trained to lead the blind, to pull wheel chairs, and to alert the deaf when an unusual sound occurs. Small monkeys are trained to act as personal aides for quadriplegics. They open and close doors, turn lights on and off, and fetch small items like keys or books when a light beam is shone on them.

(10)   Modern technology has indeed offered hope and independence to many disabled people. Sophisticated environment controls, like the ones that David Pollard activated with the movement of his eyebrow, are very expensive, but a myriad of other technological innovations are readily available for most of the disabled people who need them. Safety and environmental control devices that were unforeseen only a few years ago are becoming more practical and less expensive every year. The actual benefits of these innovations are not easily assessed, but they are far-reaching. People who 20 years ago would have been confined to a bed are now able to care for many of their own needs, pursue educational goals, and maintain jobs. Many people who were recently unable to be left alone now have devices that allow them the independence of their own homes and their own interests. As the disabled profit more from the resources of public life, society in turn benefits from their contributions. Technology has undeniably improved the prospects for the handicapped.

Comprehension Check

The purpose of this activity is to check your understanding of the article and to give practice using vocabulary words. Label each sentence true or false according to the article. If you cannot understand the meaning of a sentence, use a dictionary to look up key words.

1. David Pollard is an example of a severely disabled person who has become proficient at many survival skills.
2. A quadriplegic is more severely disabled than a paraplegic.
3. Many of the architectural renovations that accommodate disabled people were built before 1960.
4. The government refused to make the Lincoln Memorial accessible to wheelchair-bound people because of this monument's prominence in American history.
5. Medical technology has helped prolong the lives of many victims of serious accidents.
6. A person who has a spinal cord injury is always paralyzed from the neck down.
7. Schools are exempt from the laws that require architectural changes for the disabled.
8. A deaf telephone operator can monitor messages by using a Braille computer terminal.
9. Breath-activated typewriters are useful for paraplegics.
10. Modern technology enables immobile people to do a myriad of commonplace tasks that would otherwise exhaust them.

UNDERSTANDING WORDS

Vocabulary List

Verbs		Nouns	Adjectives/ Participles	Adverbials
accommodate	designate	discrimination	accessible	severely
acquire	enable	myriad	audible	vividly
activate	exhaust	prospect	commonplace	whereby
appeal	expose	renovations	exclusive	
assess	monitor	scope	exempt	
deny	paralyze	terminal	immobile	
deserve	prolong	victim	proficient	
			self-sufficient	

Subject-Specific Vocabulary

Nouns: Braille, paraplegic, quadriplegic, spinal cord.
Adjectives: able-bodied, blind, deaf, disabled, handicapped.

Activity 1

Substitute a synonym from the vocabulary list for each word or group of words in parentheses. Be sure to keep the original meaning of the sentence.

1. After the civil rights movement in the 1960s, (disabled) people began to (publicize) the fact that they were (casualties) of (prejudice).

2. As a result of the new laws that were passed in the 1970s, many buildings became (available) to wheelchairs and special parking spaces were (appointed) for the (privileged) use of handicapped people.

3. Since David Pollard's body is (paralyzed) below the neck, he must use a wheelchair that can be (started) with his breath or with slight movements of his head.

4. A person who is (unable to see) can read by using a machine that scans a printed page and turns it into words that are (capable of being heard).

5. Many disabled people have (gained) technological assistance, but others have not gotten the help they (justifiably should have had).

Activity 2

Describe the relationship between each of the following pairs of words: (antonyms, synonyms, neither).

1. prospect/impossibility
2. hinder/enable
3. self-sufficient/paid
4. proficient/prominent

5. renovation/expansion
6. immobilized/paralyzed
7. deny/acknowledge

8. appoint/designate
9. excused/exempt
10. vividly/distinctly

Activity 3

Cross out the one word that does not have the same meaning as the underlined word.

1. The doctor prolonged her time in the hospital because her condition was critical.
   a. extended   b. lengthened   c. denied   d. continued

2. The scope of his abilities wasn't understood until he started his new job.
   a. extent   b. breadth   c. range   d. value

3. A deaf person who is proficient at lip reading can often adapt to college life.
   a. coherent   b. capable   c. competent   d. skillful

4. The computer programmer discovered a myriad of details that had to be changed before the program would be effective.
   a. abundance   b. obstacle   c. large amount   d. multitude

5. Nearly everyone in my family is shy. I wonder how my sister <u>acquired</u> such an outgoing personality.
   a. obtained   b. learned   c. gained   d. got
6. His vocal cords were <u>severely</u> injured but his voice was audible.
   a. extremely   b. intensely   c. vividly   d. badly
7. The director of the library designated one room for the <u>exclusive</u> use of graduate students.
   a. privileged   b. sole   c. solitary   d. excessive
8. Computers are now <u>commonplace</u>.
   a. familiar   b. widespread   c. usual   d. insufficient

Activity 4

What renovations or adjustments would have to be made to make each of the following places accessible to a paraplegic who is wheelchair-bound? Consider as many details as possible.

a bank	a movie theater	a bar
a library	a grocery store	a 4th-floor dentist's office

Activity 5

To expose something can mean "to deliberately bring about contact" with something.

> My parents exposed me to my first ballet when I was eight years old.
> I was exposed to my first ballet when I was eight years old.

To which of the following items would you expose your five-year-old child? Explain.

violent movies	a friend with the measles	the bright sun on a hot day
classical music	people of different races	a person who uses
television		profane language

Activity 6

To expose something can also mean "to reveal or uncover something." The opposite is "to conceal or hide."

> The police exposed the fact that the actress was arrested for drunk driving, even though she tried to conceal it.

To whom would you not be willing to expose each of the following?

your income	your grade point average
your naked body	your father's occupation

Activity 7

To *deny* something can mean "to refuse to give or to withhold something."

> *Her parents denied her permission to attend college.*
> *She was denied permission to attend college.*

What are the following people likely to be denied?

1. A child misbehaves at the dinner table.
2. A student with a low grade point average applies for college.
3. While taking a driving exam, a driver hits a stop sign.
4. A child goes to a liquor store to buy a bottle of whiskey.
5. A teenager who doesn't have a job goes to a bank and wants to borrow money.

Activity 8

To *deserve* something means "to be entitled to or to be worthy of something."

> *The scientist deserved credit for the innovation.*
> *The murderer deserves a severe punishment.*

Refer again to the sentences in Activity 7. What does each of the people deserve?

Activity 9

Whereby means "by which means" or "through which."

> *The woman studied French, whereby she was able to communicate when she vacationed in France.*

Complete each of the following sentences, choosing appropriate verbs from the column on the right.

1. Mary took swimming lessons, whereby she	was able to
2. My brother found a good job, whereby he	learned
3. I earned a Masters Degree in computer science, whereby I	became
4. The blind boy studied Braille, whereby he	

Activity 10

To *assess* something can mean "to determine the ability or value of something."

> *They assessed the paraplegic girl's ability to use her legs and determined that she could learn to use crutches.*
> *The banker assessed the value of the house at $150,000.*

What would be the reason for assessing each of the following? Who would make each of these assessments?

a student's ability

the marketability of a new food product

the success of a new movie

the extent of a person's blindness

a teacher's effectiveness

the self-sufficiency of a deaf worker

Activity 11

To monitor something can mean "to listen or watch for the purpose of maintaining order or safety."

Under which circumstances would each of the following activities be monitored, and under which circumstances would each be assessed?

1. an airplane's first flight
2. a child's early attempt to walk
3. a teenager's first date
4. a teenager's ability to drive a car
5. the first time a paraplegic person uses a new wheelchair
6. the first time a guide dog assists a blind person
7. a hospital patient's heart rate.

Activity 12

Affixes can sometimes be added to adjectives or nouns to create a verb form. For example:

Prefix:	en -	+ able	= enable
Suffixes:	- ize, ise	+ popular	= popularize
	- ify	+ glory	= glorify
	- ate	+ active	= activate
	- en	+ haste	= hasten

For each of the following verb forms, underline the affix that indicates that it is a verb. Then find the related word form that is indicated in parentheses. Use your dictionary whenever necessary. The first one is done for you.

Verb form   **Base form**

1. <u>en</u>vision   _____vision_____ (noun)

2. visualize   _____ (adj)

3. mobilize   _____ (adj)

4. enliven   _____ (adj)

5. individualize   _____ (noun)

6. characterize   _____ (noun)

7. dramatize _____ (noun)

8. criticize _____ (noun)

9. theorize _____ (noun)

10. symbolize _____ (noun)

11. victimize _____ (noun)

Activity 13

To appeal can mean "to awaken a favorable response; to be interesting to someone."

Hot coffee does not appeal to me when the weather is hot.
Cartoons appeal to small children.

To whom might each of the following appeal?

a warm blanket	generic grocery	loud music
a funny movie	products	an inexpensive vacation
vivid colors	a financial venture	

Activity 14

Put a **v** in front of items that are visible, an **A** in front of items that are audible, a **B** in front of items that are both audible and visible, and an **N** in front of items that are neither audible nor visible.

a motion picture	a dripping faucet	falling snow
an ambulance siren	a frown	wind
thunder	gasoline fumes	electricity

Activity 15

In pairs or small groups, discuss the following questions.

1. What is your favorite food? Describe why it appeals to you.

2. From which of the following are you exempt?
   paying U.S. income tax   getting a marriage license
   renewing your U.S. visa   carrying a driver's license
   paying tuition

3. Handicapped people are sometimes the victims of discrimination. What other groups are discriminated against?

4. Describe a memory from your childhood that you remember vividly. Why do you think this memory has remained so vivid?

5. What special accommodations would you make if a wheelchair-bound friend were coming to your home for dinner?

6. Are any parts of your school inaccessible to a quadriplegic person? If so, what renovations are needed to make them accessible? (Consider every room and as many details as possible.)

7. Following is a list of commonplace tasks. Place them in order according to how physically exhausting they might be to a paraplegic.

making coffee	eating	dressing
buying groceries	bathing	depositing money in the bank

8. Paraphrase the title of this chapter.

PUTTING WORDS INTO SENTENCES

Ten words have been selected from the original vocabulary list for closer study. These words and their related forms are charted below.

Verbs	Nouns	Adjectives/ Participles	Adverbials
access	access accessibility	accessible	
accommodate	accommodation	accommodated accommodating	
acquire	acquisition	(un)acquired	
deny	denial	undeniable denied	undeniably
enable	ability disability	able disabled disabling	ably
exclude	exclusiveness exclusion	(un)exclusive	exclusively in exclusion of excluding
expose	exposure	exposed	
(im)mobilize	(im)mobility (im)mobilization	(im)mobile	
paralyze	paralysis	paralyzed paralyzing	
terminate	terminal	terminal	terminally

Activity 1

To *acquire* something means "to gain or to get something, sometimes as a result of one's own effort or work."

> *The doctor recently acquired a new X-ray machine, but the technician was not happy with the new acquisition.*

Imagine that your aunt was recently in a serious car accident and she needs to use a wheelchair. You recently acquired one from a hospital, and you found that it has a malfunction. Since the chair is almost new, you think the manufacturer should pay for the repairs, but before they will, you must answer their questions. Use the information in the chart to answer the questions, and include the words in parentheses in your answers.

Nature of patient's disability: Complete paralysis below the waist and partial paralysis of arms.
Cause of patient's disability: Spinal cord injury, car accident.
Date wheelchair was acquired: March 5, 19____
Acquired from: Mercy Hospital
Model: Standard Wheelchair, Model #1400
Nature of malfunction: Wheels are difficult to turn.

1. Why did you need to acquire this wheelchair? (was acquired)
2. When was the wheelchair first acquired? (acquisition)
3. From whom did you receive it, and what model is it? (acquired)
4. Describe the problem you are having with the wheelchair. (acquired, adj)
5. Did the malfunction begin before or after you purchased the wheelchair? (acquisition)

Many things besides possessions can be <u>acquired</u>, including a disease, a habit, a taste for something, a new interest, and a reputation.

AIDS (Acquired Immune Deficiency Syndrome) is a deadly disease that can be acquired through contact with contaminated blood.

I used to dislike coffee, but I acquired a taste for it when I was in college.

Activity 2

To deny something can mean "to refuse to give or allow" something.

The university denied his request for a scholarship.

It can also mean "to declare untrue" or "to refuse to accept as fact."

The driver denied that he had been involved in the car accident.

Now imagine that the manufacturer mentioned in Activity 1 has denied your request. The following letter is your objection to the denial. Read the letter, then restate the sentences, using the word forms below. You may need to add words or change the word order to make the sentences logical. After you have written the sentences, label each of them according to whether *deny* is defined by definition #1 or #2.

To Whom It May Concern:

(**a**) I was recently informed of your denial of my request for wheelchair repair, and I was very disappointed. (**b**) I don't understand why you rejected my request. (**c**) Perhaps I could have understood your rejection if the chair had been old. (**d**) However, there is no doubt that the chair is new. (**e**) I therefore request that you study your records and that you reevaluate the reason why you decided not to allow this repair.

1. (Sentence **a**)   denied
2. (Sentence **b**)   denial
3. (Sentence **c**)   denied
4. (Sentence **d**)   undeniably
5. (Sentence **e**)   was denied

Activity 3

Access refers to "the state of being available" or "being able to come near."

> *I have access to all of the books in the university library because I am a student.*

The adjective *accessibile* and the noun *accessibility* refer to the ease of availability.

> *Library books are accessible to all university students, but not all students take advantage of this accessibility.*

Imagine that you are temporarily confined to a wheelchair because of a leg injury. Write sentences about your experiences in public places, using the provided words in the given order. The first one has been done for you.

1. Upstairs offices/inaccessible/elevator

   > *Upstairs offices are inaccessible to me unless there is an elevator.*

2. Public telephones/inaccessible/high
3. access/library books/aisles
4. accessibility of/grocery store/depends on
5. public sidewalks/accessible/ramp

Activity 4

The adjectives *disabled* and *disabling* and the noun *disability* are most often used in reference to people, and usually refer to physical or mental incapacities.

> *The child described her father's disability to her teacher.*
> *The disabled veteran depended on his wheelchair.*

On the other hand, the forms *enable*, *ability*, and *ably* can be used in reference to both people and things.

> *The strong wind enabled the glider to float in the air for a long time. Its ability to catch the wind reminded us of how ably a bird can float in the breeze.*

Following is a diagram of a van that has been modified so it can be entered and operated by a person in a wheelchair. Write sentences describing this van, using the provided words in the given order. The first one has been done for you.

1. enables/paraplegic

   The wheelchair lift enables a paraplegic to enter the van while seated in the wheelchair.

2. disability/automatic door opener
3. person in a wheelchair/able/hand-operated accelerator and brake
4. exterior door opener/accessible/disabled person
5. wheelchair lockdown/driver/ability/wheelchair

Activity 5

To exclude something means "to keep out or leave out something." It is often followed by *from* and is often used in the passive form.

> *Public schools once excluded handicapped children because the schools did not have adequate facilities.*
>
> *I was excluded from the conversation because I didn't speak French.*

Create passive sentences telling who is excluded from each of these experiences. Explain why the exclusion occurs.

1. entering a bar
2. getting a driver's license
3. playing on a tennis team

Activity 6

Exclusive and *exclusively* are used to describe things that are not shared with others.

> *Some rides at the amusement park are for the exclusive enjoyment of children.*
> *The copy machine in the principal's office is reserved exclusively for teachers.*

Name something that is reserved for each of the following people or groups. Create sentences using the forms in parentheses.

1. the president of the United States (exclusive)
2. senior citizens (exclusive)
3. men (exclusively)
4. handicapped people (exclusive)

> When used colloquially, <u>exclusive</u> can refer to a place that is very expensive and sophisticated. Although anyone who can afford it can enter, it is still considered <u>exclusive</u>.
>
> We took the business client to an exclusive restaurant to create a positive impression.

Activity 7

Mobile and *mobility* refer to someone or something that has freedom of movement.

> *The computer programmer was willing to move to a different town. He was hired because of this mobility.*

Mobile often appears as a medical term referring to the ability to move, and can be used in reference to a person or to parts of the body.

> *Although my grandfather had major surgery, he was mobile only three days later.*

When *mobile* is used in reference to an object, it suggests that the object was built with the intention of being moved.

> *The truck moved the mobile home from California to Arizona.*

When something is forced to stay in one place, its effectiveness may be limited. Mobility can improve the situation in various ways. Create sentences that explain such improvements or the need for such improvements by combining the following groups of words. You may need to change the word order.

1. a hospital patient/independence/mobile
2. mobile/health care facility/convenient
3. mobility/a weather station/accuracy
4. a quadriplegic/self-confidence/mobility

> <u>Automobile</u> literally means "self-moving." This meaning has been extended to other noun forms like <u>bloodmobile</u> and <u>bookmobile.</u>
>
> The bloodmobile travels to different locations to make it convenient for people to donate blood.

Activity 8

To *mobilize* something means "to organize or to assemble something for use." The noun form *mobilization* also refers to this process.

> During the 1960s, efforts were made to mobilize the many handicapped people who formerly had been discriminated against. This mobilization had a significant impact on public policy.

Change each of the sentences below to include the words *mobile, mobility, mobilize,* or *mobilization.*

1. After the earthquake, the Red Cross organized many volunteers to help in the rescue effort.
2. This effort was successful because there were volunteers whose jobs allowed them to leave home.
3. Once they arrived at the site of the disaster, they realized that they would have a limited ability to move throughout the city because many roads were destroyed.
4. Because they had access to large earth-moving equipment, they were able to open the roads and restore the people's ability to move about the city.
5. Ultimately, these efforts to find the needed equipment and to use it to open the roads enabled many lives to be saved.

Activity 9

To *paralyze* something means "to cause something to be unable to move itself." It is primarily used in reference to parts of the body, and is often used to exaggerate personal feelings.

> As a result of the insect bite, my hand was paralyzed for two hours. I was paralyzed with fear when I first realized I couldn't move it.

To *immobilize* something means that external forces have restricted movement or the ability to move around.

> The skiing accident immobilized me for a week.
> The doctor immobilized my arm so I wouldn't irritate the sprain.

Change each of the sentences below to include the words *paralyze, paralyzed,* and *paralysis, immobilize, immobilized,* or *immobilization.* More than one answer may be appropriate.

1. As a result of the accident, the man was a quadriplegic.
2. We got off the freeway because of the traffic jam.
3. The movie was so frightening that we couldn't move.
4. The two paraplegic men played wheelchair basketball.
5. Because the child was so active, the doctor restricted the movement of his leg so he wouldn't aggravate the cut.

6. Movement within the city was stopped because of the snow storm.

7. Eating certain poisonous plants can make you unable to move your body.

Activity 10

Restate each of the sentences listed on the left, using one of the words listed on the right. Use at least one word in each sentence, making sure to use all the words listed on the right.

1. The ability to move from place to place is critical to all handicapped people.	paralyzed
	denying
2. Laws have therefore been passed that forbid airlines and other transportation companies from refusing seats to disabled people.	able
	mobility
	accessible
3. All airline personnel must know how to help handi-capped people.	accommodate
	handicap
4. Many cruise ships have rooms that can be used by travelers in wheelchairs.	
5. Some car rental agencies seek to meet the needs of drivers whose legs are immobilized by providing cars that can be driven with hand controls.	

Activity 11

To expose something can mean "to reveal, unmask," or "leave something unguarded." This definition is usually used in reference to something negative.

> *The dishonesty of the apartment managers was exposed when we found the stolen money. This exposure led to their arrest.*
> *If you expose your skin to too much sun, it will burn.*

Read the following story, then answer the questions that follow, using the words in parentheses.

Michael Monroe was a dishonest investor. He convinced many elderly people to let him invest their life savings in valuable property, but the property didn't really exist. He explained that the property was in another state so they couldn't visit it, but that it was very valuable and that they would make large profits. Instead of investing the money, he spent it on houses, cars, and vacations for himself. Mr. Ernest M. Miller was the first to discover this scam when he checked the property records and found out the truth about the real estate. Soon thereafter, the police investigated Mr. Monroe's business.

1. Who apparently exposed this crime to the police? (was exposed)

2. How did Mr. Monroe's business probably change after the facts were exposed? (exposure)

3. What do you think happened when this crime was discovered by newspaper re-porters? (exposed)

Activity 12

When *expose* is used to mean "to bring about contact with something," it can be used in reference to something either negative or positive.

> *We wanted our children to be exposed to Japanese food before we visited Japan, so we took them to a Japanese restaurant.*

Formulate a sentence that tells what can happen to each of the groups of people in Column I when they are exposed to each of the situations in Column II.

Column I	Column II
1. Americans	people from different countries
2. children	too much television violence
3. teenagers	loud rock music
4. disabled people	high technology
5. twins	different environments

To <u>over</u>expose means to expose something excessively.
To <u>under</u>expose means to expose something less than is necessary.

> The overexposed photographs were taken under a bright sun, so they turned out too light. The underexposed ones were taken in a cave, so they were too dark.

Activity 13

All forms of the word *terminal* refer to the end of something. *To terminate* can be transitive or intransitive.

> *The actress terminated her contract with the movie studio.*

To terminate can also mean "to dismiss from employment" or "to fire."

> *Susie was terminated from her job at On Time Clock Company because she was always late.*

Use either the active or passive form of *terminate* to create a sentence that indicates who might terminate each of the following, and why it was terminated.

1. an agreement between a home buyer and a home seller
2. a contract to produce a movie
3. an argument between a husband and a wife
4. a business relationship between a millionaire and a bank.
5. a teenager's employment at a fast food restaurant

> **Terminal** can mean "close to causing death."
>
> If someone has a terminal illness, that person is dying. A terminally ill person may live for several months.
>
> **Terminal** is also used to refer to either end of a transportation line (bus, train, airline, trucking, etc.).
>
> The bus terminal was crowded because three buses were late.

USING WORDS IN CONTEXT

Activity 1

Your instructor will dictate a paragraph about small monkeys that have been trained to help quadriplegics. After you have written the paragraph, work with a partner to fill in words you may have missed or to correct grammar and spelling. When you and your partner believe your paragraphs are correct, compare them to the paragraph printed at the back of the book. Make any necessary corrections.

Activity 2

Write a paragraph about specific groups of disabled people who might benefit from the special telephone in the next paragraph. The following words may help you express your ideas: accommodate, appeal, assess, enable, monitor, paralyze, myriad, audible, immobile, sufficent, severely, whereby.

Special telephones are available that allow a friend or relative to call the home of a handicapped person and to check on such environmental situations as the room temperature. Even if the person doesn't answer the phone, the caller can still hear any suspicious sounds and report them. These same devices can be pre-programmed to regularly ask the disabled person in a synthesized voice such questions as "Are you okay?" If there is no response within a few minutes, the device automatically dials the telephone and requests help.

Activity 3

Read the following paragraph as many times as you can in three minutes. Then with your book closed, rewrite as much of the information as you can remember.

Stephen Hawking is often recognized as the most brilliant physicist of the twentieth century. When he was just beginning his career, he acquired a serious nerve disease that left him almost completely paralyzed and unable to speak. Although his prospects looked hopeless, Dr. Hawking sought to continue his research and to pursue some of the most difficult questions in the world of physics. He acquired a special computer that enabled him to select words on a computer screen and to express them through an audible voice synthesizer that other people could hear. Although this process is slow, his computer enabled Hawking to become a distinguished scholar at Cambridge University. In 1988 the general population was exposed to his work when he published a book that has become a best seller and is considered to be a significant contribution to the world of physics.

Topics for Writing or Discussion

1. What problems will handicapped students (wheelchair-bound, deaf, or blind) face if they attend a university? What can the university do to help them? What can fellow students and professors do to help them? What can they do to help themselves? Consider both in-class and out-of-class activities.

2. Imagine that you are a doctor and you have been asked to write a newspaper article suggesting ways to rear a handicapped child. Write an article that is both informative and convincing.

3. You have been assigned the task of designing a public library. Write a proposal that would consider the needs of the handicapped.

8

THE FICKLE FORCES OF NATURE

ESTABLISHING A CONTEXT

Pre-reading Discussion

- Have you ever experienced an earthquake, hurricane, or other dramatic natural phenomenon?
- What are the biggest problems that nature causes in the place where you live?
- Which type of natural disaster is the most destructive?

Read this article for general meaning. If you cannot understand the meaning of the content, use a dictionary to look up key words (words that are important to the meaning).

(1)   The abundant natural resources on earth have created an environment in which humankind has been able not merely to survive but to flourish. In the relatively short time that humans have inhabited the earth, they have discovered and exploited the energy potential of sun, wind, and water power and, more recently, the energy contained in fossil fuels and atoms. Humans have hunted, foraged for, and domesticated animal and plant species to supply themselves with food and clothing. Humans have used nature's mineral resources to create machines, roads, and skyscrapers. The abundance of nature's gifts has made possible complex civilizations that are sustained by sophisticated systems of communication and transportation. Yet the gifts that fickle nature provides with one hand, it often takes away with the other hand through natural catastrophes that disrupt human activities, topple human creations, and destroy human lives. As a result, humans both respect and fear nature, for they realize that the inventiveness of human minds and the toil of human muscles are virtually powerless against the tremendous forces of nature.

(2)   Perhaps the most catastrophic natural phenomena are earthquakes, which can shake, split, and shift the ground upon which our civilizations are built. Invisible and inaudible in their approach, they strike without warning, endure for mere seconds,

A 1962 hurricane was responsible for extensive damage to the New England coast. Courtesy of NOAA (the National Oceanic and Atmospheric Administration).

and then are gone. A mild earthquake may do no more than rattle windows; a severe earthquake can devastate a city and reduce it to a pile of debris.

(3)   Earthquakes are caused by the movement of 50-mile-thick plates that comprise the earth's crust, or outer shell. More than two thousand earthquakes occur daily somewhere on our planet, but about 95 percent of them are too weak to be felt except by sensitive seismometers, instruments that measure movement within the earth. Of those that are felt by humans, most cause relatively little damage, particularly if they occur in sparsely inhabited areas. Each year, however, about ten powerful earthquakes strike somewhere on earth, causing extensive damage and loss of life.

(4)   Earthquakes are not limited geographically, but occur predominately in three locations. One area that is particularly vulnerable is where ocean plates are thrusting under land plates, as along the west coasts of Central and South America, Alaska, and the islands of Japan and Indonesia. Another is where the plates are scraping past each other, as in California and Turkey. The third is where continents are colliding with each other, as in China, Iran, and southeast Europe, which are being pressured by the northward movement of India, Arabia, and Africa, respectively.

(5)   The tremendous power of giant earthquakes is almost incomprehensible. As the earth heaves and thrusts, buildings and bridges collapse, roads buckle, train rails twist, water and gas lines burst, and power poles topple. People caught in the quake may be struck by falling objects or buried under tons of debris. A strong earthquake can virtually destroy a city in seconds, leaving thousands of people dead, injured, or homeless. For example, in 1976 a massive quake struck the city of Tangshan, China, killing an estimated 750,000 people, injuring 780,000, and leaving 500,000 without homes. Almost every multistory building in the city was either destroyed or severely damaged.

(6)   Scientists have observed that certain phenomena seem to occur before an earthquake as the pressure within the plates intensifies. Myriads of tiny cracks appear in the rock, causing it to expand and uplift the ground above it. The pressure squeezes water out of the rock, thereby raising nearby water levels. Also, the rock becomes more resistant to electric current, and radon gas is released. Scientists hope that these interrelated phenomena will provide keys to predict when and where an earthquake will occur, thereby enabling them to warn people to evacuate the area. While the earthquake itself cannot be prevented, at least lives may be saved.

(7)   Scientists theorize that movement of the earth's plates is also responsible for volcanoes. The tremendous pressure created by the plates as they collide generates sufficient heat to liquify rock located deep underground. As the pressure intensifies, the liquid rock is forced up through channels in the resistant rock to the earth's surface. There it can erupt with explosive force, burying nearby areas under tons of red-hot rock and ashes. The most violent eruption of modern times took place in 1883, when the volcanic island of Krakatoa, located between Java and Sumatra, exploded. The blast was audible nearly 3,000 miles away. Ashes from the great explosion darkened the sky over a 275-mile area, and dust remained in the earth's upper atmosphere for more than a year. A 120-foot ocean wave generated by the explosion rushed outward to inundate islands and seacoasts in its path.

(8)   Giant waves are also partially responsible for the devastation caused by hurricanes, which are called cyclones or typhoons in some parts of the world. Hurricanes originate over warm tropical seas where water temperatures exceed 80°F. There, moisture-filled air rotates upward around a relatively calm interior "eye," the most distinctive feature of hurricanes. The rising air conveys billions of tons of water vapor to cool high altitudes, where it condenses into billions of tons of rain that falls to earth. As more water-filled air is sucked in at the bottom, the storm progressively grows in size and intensity. Sometimes hurricanes are as extensive as 300 miles in diameter and have winds rotating at 200 miles per hour. As it grows, the entire storm system simultaneously travels in an unpredictable path, usually out to sea, where it will eventually dwindle. But sometimes it moves toward land, where it can bring tremendous destruction.

(9)   The erratic paths of hurricanes are traced by radar, satellites, ships at sea, aircraft, and weather balloons. When a hurricane is observed heading for land, inhabitants are warned to evacuate or to prepare themselves for the impact of the storm and the giant sea waves that will precede it. When the hurricane strikes, the high-velocity winds rip apart buildings, topple trees, and batter vehicles while the giant waves and torrential rain inundate low-lying coastal areas. Fortunately, once a hurricane travels over land it quickly dies out because of the lack of sea water to sustain its power.

(10)   The experience of one hurricane survivor illustrates what can happen when humans fail to respect the power of nature. When Hurricane Camille was headed for the U.S. coast in 1969, residents of a three-story apartment building disregarded warnings to evacuate and chose to remain for a "hurricane party." Soon after the party started, a 25-foot-high wall of water surged on shore; then heavy rain struck. Within a short time, rising water reached the second-story windows of the apartment building. Suddenly the building collapsed, and 24 of the 25 party-goers were drowned. The only survivor was found the next morning high in a tree top four miles from where the apartment building had been.

(11)   At that time, Hurricane Camille was considered the most destructive hurricane ever to hit the United States, with 250 people dead, 80 missing, and roughly one-half billion dollars in property damage. However tragic the losses, they are insignificant compared to losses from other storms: 300,000 drowned in Calcutta in a 1737 cyclone; 300,000 killed in China by a typhoon in 1881; and 500,000 killed by a cyclone in Bangladesh in 1970. One reason for the large number of deaths is that coastal areas vulnerable to hurricanes are among the most densely inhabited areas in the world.

(12)   It is hard to envision a more powerful storm than a hurricane, yet nature's strongest storms are not hurricanes but tornadoes. Although a tornado is smaller than a hurricane, it can do more damage in a shorter time than a hurricane. Tornadoes occur throughout the world, but they strike with greatest frequency in the United States. About 600 tornadoes occur there annually, usually in the spring and summer when warm, moist air flowing northward from the Gulf of Mexico collides with cold, dry air flowing southward from polar regions. The cold air thrusts the warm air violently upward to form a massive thunderstorm system within which a rotating wind develops. As the wind intensifies in velocity, it forms a characteristic funnel-shaped spi-

ral beneath the black cloud mass. Within the hollow interior of this funnel-shaped cloud, a partial vacuum is created by the rapidly rotating winds that can reach an estimated 500 miles per hour. If the tip of the swirling funnel cloud touches the ground, devastation is inevitable. Only the strongest steel-and-concrete structures are sufficiently resistant to the wind to remain standing, and even these will probably suffer some damage from flying debris caught in the wind.

(13)   The swirling tornado can pick up houses and cars and fling them down again. The low pressure within the funnel can also cause houses to literally explode because of the relatively higher air pressure within the houses. The high-velocity winds have been known to drive a pencil through a tree trunk and to pluck the feathers off chickens. Yet because of the narrow, erratic path of a tornado, it is not uncommon for one house to be totally destroyed while its neighbor is left untouched.

(14)   The same weather conditions that generate tornadoes also generate lightning. Since ancient times, humans have been awed by lightning. Indeed, the spectacular flashes of light that streak through the skies are worthy of wonderment. Flashes of lightning are actually channels of electrical energy that travel from the ground to the clouds at the speed of 90,000 miles per second. As the energy travels upward, it heats the surrounding air to a temperature of 50,000°F. and delivers 125 million volts of electricity. The tremendous heat causes the air to expand rapidly, generating massive shock waves audible as thunder.

(15)   Roughly 8 million lightning flashes blast the earth every day, which is about 100 every second. Most do no harm, but each year lightning is responsible for starting about half of all U.S. forest fires and causing millions of dollars' worth of property damage. Lightning also disrupts electric power service when it strikes electric transformers, causing them to burst from the sudden increase in energy.

(16)   Whereas some catastrophes are instantaneous, others, such as droughts, are cumulative. Extended periods of insufficient rainfall prevent farmers from growing food to sustain their families or to market for profit. When nature fails to provide enough rain, humans can no longer exploit the land, and they must either leave their homes for more fertile areas or starve to death. Those who do manage to survive face undernourishment and disease.

(17)   Throughout most of the 1930s, the seasonal rains failed to fall on normally productive farmlands in the central United States, resulting in a severe drought known as the "Dust Bowl." Crops could not grow, and cattle suffocated from terrible dust storms or starved from lack of feed. Rich topsoil was blown away by hot, dry winds, which subsequently left the land infertile for years. The human suffering that resulted from this catastrophe was dramatized by John Steinbeck in his classic novel *The Grapes of Wrath*.

(18)   The natural catastrophes that take place on earth are cruel reminders of nature's fickle character. Nature both provides and takes away. No matter how sophisticated our technology becomes, we will probably always be vulnerable to the awesome forces of nature.

Comprehension Check

The purpose of this activity is to check your understanding of the article and to give practice using vocabulary words. Label each sentence true or false according to the article. If you cannot understand the meaning of a sentence, use a dictionary to look up key words.

1. Areas most vulnerable to droughts are located along densely inhabited seacoasts.
2. High-velocity winds are responsible for the tremendous devastation caused by tornadoes.
3. Lightning occurs when warm, moist air collides with cold, dry air.
4. The intensity of a hurricane increases as its path crosses over land.
5. Unlike typhoons, hurricanes originate over warm tropical seas.
6. Scientists hope to prevent earthquakes by studying the phenomena that occur before earthquakes strike.
7. Earthquakes are the only type of catastrophe powerful enough to cause buildings to collapse.
8. The sound of thunder generates shock waves that heat the air to 50,000°F.
9. Volcanic eruptions generate sufficient pressure to cause movement of the earth's plates.
10. Roughly half of all U.S. forest fires originate from lightning strikes.

UNDERSTANDING WORDS

Vocabulary List

Verbs	Nouns	Adjectives/Participles	Adverbials
burst	catastrophe	erratic	densely
collapse	debris	extensive	sparsely
collide	intensity	fickle	upward
destroy	path	moist	
disrupt	pressure	located	
dwindle	velocity	resistant	
endure		responsible (for)	
exploit		rotating	
flourish		tremendous	
generate		vulnerable	
inhabit			
originate			
prevent			
provide			
sustain			

Subject-Specific Vocabulary

Verbs: erupt, evacuate, devastate, strike.   **Nouns:** altitude, atmosphere, wave.

Activity 1

Substitute a synonym from the vocabulary list for each word or group of words in parentheses.

1. When a hurricane is about to (hit) a seacoast, people who (live in) the area are warned to (leave) or to prepare for the storm.
2. To prepare their houses, people cover the windows with boards to (stop) them from being broken by the (force) of the high-(speed) winds.
3. People store enough drinking water and food to (support) them for a few days.
4. They also need to (furnish) emergency lighting and cooking equipment because the storm may (interfere with) electric and gas service for a/an (lengthy) period after the storm passes.
5. People are warned to remain indoors for as long as the (great) winds (last).
6. Anyone outdoors in a hurricane is (exposed) to injury from flying (trash).
7. The giant sea waves and heavy rainfall that hurricanes (produce) can cause buildings to (fall down).
8. A powerful hurricane can (totally destroy) an area before it (decreases) and moves away.

Activity 2

To generate and *to originate* are similar in meaning. *To generate* something means "to produce something" and is a transitive verb. *To originate* means "to begin" and is most commonly used in the intransitive form.

> *Tornadoes generate high winds.*
> *Hurricanes originate over warm seas.*

Complete each sentence with *generate* or *originate*.

1. High-altitude weather satellites _____ photographs of weather systems on earth.
2. Volcanic eruptions _____ deep underground.
3. Meteorologists do not completely understand how hurricanes _____.
4. Undersea earthquakes _____ tremendous sea waves called "tsunamis."
5. As radium breaks down, it _____ radon gas.

Activity 3

Put an **H** before each statement that describes hurricanes and a **T** before each statement that describes tornadoes. Put a **B** if a statement describes both hurricanes and tornadoes.

have rotating winds	originate over warm seas
have erratic paths	inundate coastlines
have narrow paths	draw water upward
have high-velocity winds	generate tremendous ocean waves

Activity 4

Cross out the one word that does not have the same meaning as the other three words.

1. The (fickle/changeable/inconsistent/helpful) behavior of nature both (supports/maintains/produces/sustains) life and destroys it.

2. If the (course/rotation/path/route) of a hurricane is directed toward cooler ocean waters, the storm will (decrease/dwindle/endure/diminish).

3. The (revolving/rotating/turning/disabling) winds of hurricanes and tornadoes move in a clockwise direction in the Southern Hemisphere and in a counterclockwise direction in the Northern Hemisphere.

4. In 1958, an earthquake in Chile (determined/generated/produced/created) a (spontaneous/tremendous/massive/enormous) sea wave that would strike the coast of Japan 22 hours later.

5. If drought conditions (acquire/endure/last/continue) for very long, crops cannot (grow/flourish/cultivate/thrive) because the soil will not be (moist/wet/damp/fertile).

6. Antarctica is one of the most sparsely inhabited areas on earth, while Japan is one of the most (heavily/widely/densely/thickly) inhabited areas.

7. (Unpredictable/irregular/intense/erratic) wind conditions increase the potential of forest fires to (damage/destroy/immobilize/devastate) a forest.

8. If lightning (impacts/strikes/hits/erupts) a tree, the tree can (burst/explode/break apart/survive).

9. Weather satellites (observe/provide/give/supply) information about weather conditions over (widespread/isolated/broad/extensive) areas.

10. A heavy snowstorm can cause roofs to (collide/collapse/fall in/cave in) and can (interrupt/exhaust/interfere with/disrupt) telephone and electric services.

Activity 5

Debris (pronounced deb-rē′) is worthless remains left over after something has been used up or destroyed.

> Careless hikers litter the trail with debris such as candy wrappers, soft-drink cans, and paper cups.

What kind of debris is likely to remain after the following events?

1. a New Year's party
2. a political convention
3. the construction of a new house
4. an airplane crash

Activity 6

To prevent something means "to keep it from occurring." What do people do to prevent the following?

1. bad luck
2. sun burns
3. milk from spoiling
4. their dogs from running away
5. head colds

Activity 7

To be responsible for something means "to cause" something.

> Careless campers are responsible for littering national forests with debris.

Look up the words below in a dictionary. Tell what damage each might be responsible for in a forest.

1. vandals
2. arsonists
3. poachers

Activity 8

To be responsible for something also refers to being assigned a job or task. Usually this meaning applies to humans or human activities.

> Forest rangers are responsible for preventing forest fires.

What is each of these workers responsible for preventing?

1. air traffic controllers
2. life guards
3. police departments
4. public health agencies
5. prison guards
6. test proctors

> Smokey the Bear, a large, friendly-looking brown bear dressed in trousers and a hat, symbolizes fire prevention in the United States. His motto is "Only you can prevent forest fires."

Activity 9

Each of the materials below is *resistant* to one or more of the forces listed on the right. What is each material resistant to? More than one answer may be possible.

Material	Force
1. wood	fire
2. iron	electrical currents
3. plastic	insect damage
4. glass	breakage
5. cement	

Activity 10

The following instruments measure either pressure or velocity. Look the words up in a dictionary and find what each instrument measures.

1. anemometer   3. speedometer
2. barometer   4. sphygmomanometer

Activity 11

An object may *burst* if the pressure inside becomes so great that the object suddenly breaks apart to release the pressure. What could cause the following to burst?

1. a balloon   4. a dam
2. a blood vessel   5. a water blister on a finger
3. a popcorn kernel   6. the seam of trousers

To burst is used figuratively to indicate an extreme amount.
> The house was bursting with people.
> The children were bursting with excitement.

To burst out means ''to react emotionally or to say something suddenly and spontaneously.''
> She burst out, ''I hate you!''

Activity 12

To *explode* means about the same as *to burst*, but *explode* suggests greater violence and a loud noise. Which of the items listed in Activity 11 could explode? *To erupt* is also similar to *burst* but usually suggests an outpouring of liquid or other material. Which of the items in Activity 11 could erupt?

What do you think is meant by the following expressions?

1. He burst out laughing.
2. The child burst into tears.
3. The audience burst into applause.
4. With a burst of speed, the car drove away.
5. He exploded with anger.
6. Cheers erupted from the crowd.

Activity 13

A *catastrophe* is an event that causes extensive damage and large loss of life or an event that will have serious effects on future lives.

Which of the following fictitious headlines might refer to a catastrophe?

1. OIL TANKERS COLLIDE; 800 MILES OF COAST COVERED WITH OIL

2. HURRICANE STRIKES UNINHABITED ISLANDS

3. 1500 HOMES DEVASTATED WHEN DAM BURSTS

4. NUCLEAR PLANT RADIATION LEAK CONTAMINATES CITY

5. UNDERSEA VOLCANIC ERUPTION CREATES NEW ISLANDS IN PACIFIC

> People often exaggerate by using catastrophe conversationally to describe an unsuccessful effort or one filled with many problems.
> I had my first job interview yesterday. It was a catastrophe.

Activity 14

When two objects *collide*, at least one of them is moving. It is named first.

The race car collided with a fence.

When both objects are moving at about the same speed and both are responsible for the collision, they can be named together.

A truck and a bus collided as they left the parking area.

When two objects collide and both are moving, the one moving faster or the one responsible for the collision is named first.

The jogger collided with the elderly woman walking her dog.

Match one object from the left column with one from the right column and tell what collided.

1. the luxury ship *Titanic*
2. a skier
3. a meteor
4. a parked car

the earth
a bicycle rider
an iceberg
a skier

Activity 15

To *strike*, when used as an intransitive verb, means "to happen or occur" and usually refers to unfortunate events that happen suddenly and unexpectedly.

If an earthquake strikes, hide under a table.

Which of these phenomena might strike?

1. a tornado
2. a thunderstorm
3. a headcold
4. summer
5. a headache
6. sunshine
7. a *tsunami*
8. cancer

> If the verb <u>strike</u> is used in a sentence with a human subject and object, it suggests hitting in anger with the hands.
> The argument ended when Fred struck Sam.

Activity 16

In a scientific sense, a *wave* is cyclical energy. A sequence of waves has a general form like ∿∿∿∿. In a nonscientific sense, a wave is a period of extreme amounts.

Match each type of wave with its description or example.

1. light waves	strike beaches
2. waves of fear	penetrate solid objects
3. ocean waves	have a velocity of 600 miles per hour
4. heat waves	unusually warm weather
5. radio waves	occur with fright
6. X-ray waves	have a velocity of 186,000 miles per second
7. sound waves	convey broadcasts

Activity 17

Erratic and *fickle* are similar in meaning and are sometimes interchangeable. *Erratic* means "having no fixed pattern," while *fickle* means "likely to change loyalties" and is often considered an undesirable personality trait.

Use *erratic* or *fickle* in each sentence.

1. The patient's rhythmic heartbeat suddenly became _____.

2. Fred loved every girl he met and wasn't true to any of them. His friends considered him _____.

3. Consumers are _____. They buy one brand of food for a long time, but when a market offers a bargain on a generic product, they buy it.

4. The insect's flight around the room was so _____ that I couldn't tell where it would fly next.

5. The weather is _____ in June. One day it's sunny, and the next day it's cold. We just can't predict it.

Activity 18

Complete each sentence with vocabulary words that are opposite in meaning.

1. The bark of redwood trees is so thick that the trees are _____ to insects. Most trees, however, are _____ to attack by insects, which can cause great damage.

2. At low altitudes, you will find thick forests _____ covering mountainsides, but as you climb upward, you will find fewer trees. At high altitudes, mountainsides are _____ covered.

3. Elephants used to _____ in Africa before humans began exploiting them for their ivory. Now their numbers have started to _____.

4. Some people _____ seacoast towns all year long, whereas vacationers live there for the summer and then _____ the towns when summer ends.

5. Mild weather with plenty of sun and rain will _____ the formation of fruit on trees, but a sudden change in the weather can _____ fruit formation.

6. Structures built by the ancient Egyptians can _____ for centuries, but modern buildings seem to _____ in a few years.

Activity 19

In pairs or in small groups, discuss the following questions.

1. The wheels of a car rotate as the car moves. What other machines or equipment have rotating parts?

2. Identify the country, continent, or area on earth that the following animals inhabit.
   a. giraffes
   b. penguins
   c. kangaroos
   d. pandas
   e. llamas
   f. whales
   g. rattlesnakes
   h. polar bears

3. The Mississippi River is located in the United States. Where is each of these geographical features located? Give the country, continent, or ocean.

   a. the Hawaiian Islands
   b. the Amazon River
   c. the Sahara Desert
   d. Mount Fuji
   e. the South Pole
   f. the Rocky Mountains
   g. the Ganges River
   h. the Grand Canyon

4. Under what conditions would the following flourish?

   weeds   your bank account   a new restaurant

5. How are the following expressions related to the article in this chapter?

   Time and tide wait for no man.
   An ounce of prevention is worth a pound of cure.

6. Explain the title of this chapter.

7. Explain the diagram below.

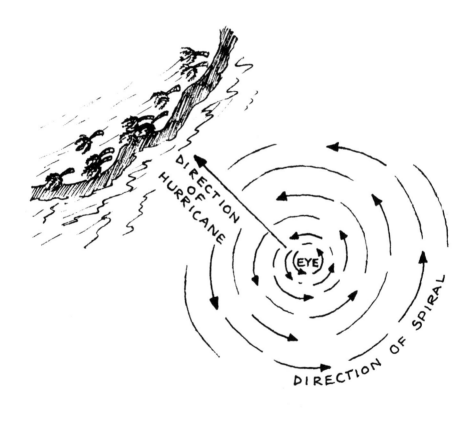

PUTTING WORDS INTO SENTENCES

Ten words have been selected from the original vocabulary list for closer study. These words and their related forms are listed below.

Verbs	Nouns	Adjectives/ Participles	Adverbials
destroy	destruction	destructive (in)destructible	destructively
endure	endurance durability duration	enduring durable endurable	
exploit	exploitation	exploitive	
extend	extension extent	extensive extended	extensively to what extent
inhabit	inhabitant habitation habitat	(un)inhabited (un)inhabitable	
intensify	intensity intensification	intense intensive	intensely intensively
originate	origin origination originator	(un)original	originally
prevent	prevention	preventable preventive	
provide	provision	provided	provided (that) provisionally
resist	resistance	resistant (ir)resistible	

Activity 1

Read the paragraph below, then restate the sentences, using the word forms given. You may need to add words or change the word order to make the sentences logical.

(a) About half of all forest fires are caused by lightning.   (b) Such fires cannot be prevented.   (c) The remaining forest fires are caused by people, either accidentally or deliberately.   (d) Strict rules can help prevent forest fires caused by people. (e) Forbidding campfires in dry forests is one way that forest fires can be prevented. (f) Another measure is to forbid smoking outside of buildings.   (g) Prohibiting visitors in forests during extremely dry seasons is an effective technique to prevent forest fires.

1. (Sentence **b**) preventable
2. (Sentence **d**) prevention
3. (Sentence **e**) prevent
4. (Sentence **f**) preventive
5. (Sentence **g**) prevented

Activity 2

Write sentences about fire prevention in the home by using the word groups below. You may have to change the word order or add words to make the sentences grammatical and logical.

1. prevention/home/save lives/fire/property
2. matches/young children/prevented/fires/keeping
3. fireplaces/fires/sparks/preventable/screens
4. fires/removing/heaters and stoves/curtains/prevent
5. best/measures/homeowners/installing/preventive/smoke alarms

Activity 3

To destroy something is to put an end to it or to make it useless.

> *Insects can destroy farm crops.*

Read the paragraph below, then restate the sentences using the word forms given. You may need to add words or change the word order to make the sentences logical.

(a) Most people who visit natural forest areas for recreation are careful, considerate people who respect nature and the rights of others to enjoy the outdoors. (b) However, some visitors are careless and cause damage. (c) Vandalism, or deliberately ruining property, is a major problem in national forests. (d) Each year, millions of dollars' worth of damage is done by vandals who attack picnic tables, signs, and restrooms with knives, spray paint, and gun shots with the intention of doing damage. (e) Some damage can be prevented by using materials that are virtually resistant to attack, such as cement, to build tables, signs, and restrooms. (f) However, it is nearly impossible to protect trees from vandals, who kill them by pulling off branches or chopping them down. (g) What a shame that the beauty of the outdoors can be ruined by the harmful behavior of a few visitors.

1. (Sentence **b**)   destructive
2. (Sentence **c**)   destruction
3. (Sentence **d**)   destructively
4. (Sentence **e**)   indestructible
5. (Sentence **f**)   destroy
6. (Sentence **g**)   destroy/destructive

Activity 4

A *habitat* is the natural environment of a living creature.

> *The habitat of gray kangaroos is the low prairies of Australia.*

A *habitation* is a dwelling place.

> *Some birds build habitations of mud and sticks.*

A place is *inhabited* if someone lives there. It is *uninhabited* if no one lives there. If conditions are such that no one is able to live in a place, then the place is *uninhabitable*. There are no *inhabitants*.

> *Before the drought, the area was densely inhabited. Now the area is so dry that it is uninhabitable.*

Complete the following sentences with the words *habitat, habitation, inhabitant, inhabit, (un)inhabited,* and *(un)inhabitable.*

1. An interesting relative of the squirrel family is the prairie dog, which _____ the western United States.

2. Prairie dogs live in large underground _____.

3. Up to 15 animals _____ one hole, with each _____ having an individual sleeping den that is connected to a large central tunnel.

4. In the past, thousands of prairie dog _____ were constructed close together and formed a "town."

5. Prairie dog towns were _____ by millions of prairie dogs and extended for hundreds of miles.

6. Prairie dog towns began to disappear as humans moved into an area, built roads and cities, and took over the _____ of the prairie dogs.

7. Once their former _____ became _____ for them, the prairie dogs moved to remote _____ areas, far from human cities, to build new towns.

8. Unfortunately, large open spaces are scarce, so the new towns are smaller and have fewer _____.

Activity 5

The information below shows the population density of eight countries of the world.

Country	Density per Square Mile	Country	Density per Square Mile
Bangladesh	2028	Japan	844
Egypt	141	Mongolia	3
France	252	Saudi Arabia	15
India	658	United States	68

Source: U.N. Demographic Yearbook, 1988.

Using the following phrases, formulate sentences about the data. The first one has been done for you.

(the least) (the most) densely inhabited
(less) (more) densely inhabited
(the most) sparsely inhabited

1. Japan: *Japan is densely inhabited.*
2. Mongolia
3. France and the United States
4. Saudi Arabia
5. Egypt and India
6. Bangladesh

Activity 6

To resist something can mean "to oppose or to fight against something."

> *Whenever he resists the temptation to overeat, he is proud of himself. He is proud when he has resistance.*

To resist something can also mean "to remain unchanged or unharmed by something."

> *Redwood trees are able to resist insect attack.*
> *Redwood trees are resistant to insect attack.*

When something is *irresistible*, it is too powerful or too pleasant to be ignored or opposed.

> *The powerful thrusts of earthquakes are irresistible, and rocks soon weaken and crack.*
> *The hungry child found the candy irresistible, and she ate it all.*

Restate each of the following sentences, using the words in parentheses.

1. The bee is an insect that can be found in virtually every part of the world; it is able to withstand all climatic extremes except those found at the North and South Poles. (resist)
2. Because most bees live and work in large groups, they are able to endure the attacks of many of their enemies. (resistance)
3. If a bee colony is disturbed, the bees fight by attacking and stinging anything that moves. (resist)
4. The bee's habitation is an intricate honeycomb that has waterproof walls that are able to sustain 30 times their weight. (resistant)
5. Bears and ants are enemies to the bees because they are strongly attracted to the sweet honey and will destroy a beehive in their pursuit of it. (irresistible)
6. Thousands of bees die every year because they are unable to tolerate the poisons that farmers use to kill other insects. (resistant)

Activity 7

To *endure* has two meanings. In its intransitive form, it means "to continue or last." In its transitive form, it means "to bear, tolerate, or suffer without giving in."

> *The great Egyptian pyramids have endured for thousands of years.*
> *The pyramids have endured earthquakes, floods, and other disasters.*

Restate the following sentences to include the word *endure*. The first one has been done for you.

1. Without oxygen, a human will die in four to six minutes.

   A human cannot endure more than four to six minutes without oxygen.

2. Camels inhabit hot, dry deserts and can go for days without water.

3. Eskimos in frigid polar areas keep warm by wearing thick fur clothing.

4. Severe winters cause food shortages for forest animals like deer.

Activity 8

To *endure* has several forms, all related in some way to lasting over time or to tolerating something. *Durable* and *durability* mean "not easily worn out or destroyed."

> *Levis blue jeans are known for their durability.*

Endurance and *(un)endurable* refer to the ability to tolerate.

> *My headache is bad, but the pain is endurable.*

Enduring means "lasting a long time."

> *Shakespeare's plays are enduring classics.*

A *duration* is a continuous period of time.

> *Temperatures in Iowa were above normal for a duration of three years.*

Use one of the above words in each space to complete the following paragraph.

Noise pollution is an invisible danger in our world. When human ears are exposed to high-decibel noises for a long _____, both psychological and physical harm can result. Decibel levels in the 20–80 range are _____ for most people, whereas levels of 120 are _____ and actually cause pain and damage to the ear. Industry considers 90 decibels the critical level of _____ for human ears. Workers exposed to _____ noise levels of 90 decibels on the job are required to wear ear protectors. As examples of sound intensities, a helicopter overhead has a decible level of 72, a ringing telephone 83, a police siren 104, and some rock bands 120. The _____ of the delicate cells inside the ear is limited. High-decibel noises can destroy them and cause permanent hearing loss.

Activity 9

Restate each of the following sentences to include the word in parentheses. The first one has been done for you.

1. Hurricane tracking and reporting are relatively recent because they depend on rapid communication. (origin)

> *Hurricane tracking and reporting are of relatively recent origin because they depend on rapid communication.*

2. Hurricanes used to be identified by the place where they started. (origination)

3. The idea of giving names to individual hurricanes first appeared in a 1941 novel. (originated)

4. The practice was adopted by the U.S. National Hurricane Center, which maintains five rotating lists of names in alphabetical order. After five hurricane seasons, the first list is used again. (original)

5. In 1984, for example, the first hurricane in the Atlantic Ocean was named Ana, the second Bob, and successive ones Claudette, David, Elena, and so on. (to originate)

6. Only female names were used until 1979, when male names were added. (originally)

7. If a hurricane has been particularly destructive, its name is withdrawn and another name substituted in the list of names. (original)

Activity 10

To provide something means "to supply something."

> *Satellites provide commercial fishing fleets with data about the location of big schools of fish.*
> *Fishing fleets depend on satellites for the provision of data on fishing locations.*

Write sentences that combine the information given. Do not change the word order of the given words. Use *provide* or *provision* in each sentence. The first one has been done for you.

1. seismometers/scientists/earthquakes

> *Seismometers provide scientists with data on earthquakes.*

2. astronomers/radio telescopes/outer space
3. cities/hydroelectric plants/electricity
4. fossil fuels/energy/factories
5. grains/dependable food supply/most underdeveloped countries

Activity 11

To provide for something means "to foresee" or "to take action for special circumstances." *To make provisions for* has the same meaning.

> People in the path of a hurricane must provide for possible food shortages after the storm. They must make provisions for water shortages, too.

Write sentences that combine the information given. Use *provide for* or *make provisions for* in each sentence. You may change the order of the information or the word forms if necessary. The first one has been done for you.

1. hurricane forecasters/erratic winds/predicting where a hurricane will strike

   > Hurricane forecasters must provide for erratic winds when they predict where a hurricane will strike.

2. architects/designing new buildings/people in wheelchairs
3. calendars/add an extra day every four years/an extra quarter-day every year
4. people have no transportation/supply buses to transport them/earthquake evacuation plans
5. first aid supplies/hikers/medical emergencies

Activity 12

Provided (that) means "on the condition (that)" or "if." In sentences, the phrase introduces a dependent clause. Sometimes *providing* is used instead.

> Lightning strikes are harmless provided that they don't hit people, animals, or objects.

Complete the following sentence with your own ideas.

1. Hurricane warnings can save lives provided that _____
2. Nation A might offer economic assistance to Nation B following a catastrophe provided that _____
3. Forests that suffer fire damage will flourish again in about 30 years provided that

   _____
4. Atomic power plants are safe provided that _____
5. Wilderness areas can be kept beautiful providing that _____

Activity 13

To exploit something means "to use something for selfish purposes or for profit." It also means "to take advantage of." The word is often used in a negative way.

> Dishonest companies exploit their customers by offering poor-quality merchandise at high prices.

To exploit can also suggest cleverness, especially with regard to business opportunities.

> *Clothing manufacturers have exploited the current interest in physical fitness by making fashionable exercise clothes.*

Read the paragraph below, then restate each numbered sentence three different ways, using the given words.

(a) Environmentalists are people who are concerned about preserving the natural state of the environment. (b) They recognize that the resources of earth are limited and need to be protected against businesses and industries. (c) Environmentalists criticize oil companies, commercial fishermen, mining companies, and loggers that use natural resources without regard for the damage they do. (d) They fear these businesses will destroy our earth.

Sentence **b**: 1. exploitation by
2. exploitive
3. that exploit the environment
Sentence **c**: 4. exploitation by
5. exploitive
6. that exploit natural resources
Sentence **d**: 7. exploitation by
8. exploitive
9. will exploit and

Activity 14

To extend means "to spread or increase in time or space." It can be used as both a transitive and intransitive verb.

> *The United States extends from the Pacific Ocean to the Atlantic Ocean.*

An *extension* is something added or drawn out.

> *My driver's license has expired. I need an extension.*

Extensive and *extensively* mean "widespread" or "over a great area."

> *The earthquake caused extensive damage.*

To what extent means "how much" and is often used with unanswered questions.

> *Scientists don't know to what extent earthquakes and volcanoes are related.*

Read the paragraph below, then answer the questions that follow in complete sentences, using the given words.

Until recently, there were over one million square miles of dense tropical forests in Brazil. However, widespread exploitation of the forests has taken place since the

1970s. Settlers have extended civilization into the once sparsely inhabited forests and have damaged them. It is not known how much of the Brazilian forests have been destroyed. In the state of Rondonia more than 20 percent of the trees have been burned or chopped down to create roads, towns, and farms. If the destruction continues at the present rate, the forests in Rondonia will be totally destroyed in 25 years. No one can foresee precisely how the destruction of the forests will affect the earth, but scientists theorize that the tremendous loss of oxygen-producing green plants will affect the earth's atmosphere.

1. Until recently, how much of Brazil was covered with tropical forests? (extended)
2. What has happened to the forests since the 1970s? (extensively)
3. What has damaged the sparsely inhabited forests? (extension)
4. How much of the Brazilian forests have been destroyed? (extent)
5. What is the extent of damage in Rondonia? (so extensive that)
6. How will the destruction of forests affect the earth? (to what extent)

Activity 15

Intensity is energy or strength and is used to describe qualities such as heat, cold, color, sound, light, and pressure.

The intensity of sound is measured in decibels.

To intensify is to grow stronger. *Intensification* is the process of growing stronger.

High humidity intensifies the discomfort of hot weather.

Intense/intensely mean ''extreme/extremely'' or ''strong/strongly.''

The intense heat of the fire forced the firefighters back. The fire was intensely hot.

Intensive/intensively mean ''to a great degree or concentration.''

Firefighters receive intensive training in life-saving techniques. They are intensively trained.

The Modified Mercalli Scale and the Richter Scale are two systems for measuring the intensity of earthquakes. The two scales are difficult to compare because they measure two different things. The Richter Scale measures the intensity of earthquakes in terms of earth movement, while the Mercalli Scale measures the intensity of earthquakes in terms of effects. Table 8.1 is a rough comparison of the two scales. It shows what effects could be expected in a densely inhabited area with various intensities of earth movement. As an example, the October 1989 San Francisco earthquake measured 7.1 on the Richter Scale and between VI and IX on the Mercalli Scale in various parts of the city. The most powerful quake ever measured was the 9.5 quake that occurred in Chile in 1960.

Look at Table 8.1, then answer the questions that follow.

Table 8.1   Earthquake Measurements

Modified Mercalli Scale	Richter Scale
I Usually not felt.	1
II Felt on upper floors of tall buildings.	2
III Felt by most people indoors.	
IV Sleepers awakened. Windows rattle.	3
V Small objects topple. Windows break.	4
VI Felt by all. Heavy furniture moved.	
VII Considerable damage to poorly built structures.	5
VIII Some structures partially collapse.	
IX Earthquake-resistant structures damaged.	
X Rails bent. Ordinary structures destroyed.	6
XI Severe damage to all structures.	7
XII Total destruction.	8
	9

1. If you heard a radio news report that said, "Last night, sleepers were awakened and windows rattled when an earthquake struck Los Angeles," what measurements would you expect the quake to have on both the Richter and Mercalli scales? (intensity)

2. The complete Mercalli descriptions also include the emotional reactions of people to an earthquake. What emotion would people probably feel in a IX earthquake? (intense)

3. What do the numbers 1–9 represent on the Richter Scale? (intensification)

4. Why would a II earthquake probably be felt only by people on the upper floors of tall buildings? (intensify)

5. The Mercalli rating is highest at the point of origin of a quake and dwindles at increasing distances from the point of origin. Why is this so? (intensive)

USING WORDS IN CONTEXT

Activity 1

The following groups of sentences are in scrambled order. Put them in the correct order by numbering them. When the sentence groups are read in the correct order, they will result in a coherent paragraph.

_____ a. Japan, a densely inhabited country, is bursting with people. Cities have extended outward and upward to their limits.

_____ b. Comfort is not the only consideration, however. The underground cities must also be safe.

_____ c. An out-of-control fire could trap thousands of people underground. To prevent such a catastrophe, sensitive smoke detectors would be installed throughout. If a fire originated, people would be immediately evacuated upward or sheltered in a pressurized temporary waiting room.

_____ d. In the future, they may extend downward. Developers envision future underground cities of stores, offices, hotels, and theaters extending for hundreds of miles.

_____ e. To make the artificial environment appear more natural, real sunlight would be reflected from the surface, and abundant green plants would flourish everywhere.

_____ f. These underground cities would be sustained by immense underground structures containing equipment to generate power, process wastes, and condition the air.

_____ g. Planners predict that the biggest obstacle to future underground cities will be psychological resistance to living underground. They fear people may be unable to endure for days without seeing the real world.

_____ h. The underground atmosphere would be carefully controlled to provide comfortable levels of temperature and humidity and to create the illusion of a natural environment.

_____ i. Engineers are confident that the structures would be safe. They would be resistant to earthquake and water leakage, and would not collapse from external pressure. Engineers admit that the structures would be vulnerable to fires.

_____ j. Therefore, planners foresee few underground habitations. Instead, people would live above ground, but work, shop, and enjoy themselves underground. Underground cities may be a good solution to Japan's shortage of space for expansion.

Activity 2

Read the following paragraph as many times as you can in three minutes. Then with your book closed, rewrite as much of the information as you can remember.

Alaska is a land of tremendous natural beauty and abundant natural resources. Environmentalists want to protect the natural beauty and prevent the exploitation of the resources. Their concern for Alaska was dramatized in 1989 when an enormous oil spill extended over 800 miles of the coastline. The oil spill occurred when an Exxon oil tanker collided with underwater rocks and the ship's tanks erupted, spilling 10 million gallons of thick, black oil near the shore. The oil devastated the beauty of the shore and destroyed the habitats of sea animals, birds, and fish. Environmentalists criticized Exxon for the accident because it was preventable. They also criticized the erratic clean-up efforts for being ineffective. They claimed that the full impact of the catastrophe may not be known for years.

Activity 3

Your instructor will dictate a paragraph about cold weather in Alaska. After you have written the paragraph, work with a partner to fill in words you may have missed or to correct grammar and spelling. When you and your partner believe your paragraphs are correct, compare them to the paragraph printed at the back of the book. Make any necessary corrections.

Topics for Writing or Discussion

1. If scientists are ever able to predict earthquakes accurately, large cities could be evacuated to protect the inhabitants from danger. If you were a member of an earthquake evacuation committee in a city of a million people, what things would you need to consider in planning for a possible evacuation?

2. Industries have been accused of destroying the environment. They use up resources and pollute the atmosphere and the waters of the earth. Which industry do you think has been the most harmful to the environment? Why?

3. One of the major problems facing modern society is disposing of its trash: the cans, bottles, plastic toys, magazines, etc., that have been used and discarded. What suggestions do you have for disposing of trash without harming the environment?

4. Describe an experience in which you faced an extreme force of nature, such as a flood or an earthquake.

APPENDIX

DICTATIONS

Chapter 1

The enormous size of the English language is reflected in the 1989 edition of the *Oxford English Dictionary*, which was published in England. Its 59 million words occupy twelve volumes. The revised edition represents five years of work. The twelve-volume first edition appeared in 1933, followed by four supplements between 1972 and 1986. The publishers say that the language has expanded by at least 450 words a year. New words that have been contributed include biofeedback, acid rain, microchip, and plastic money from the fields of medicine, ecology, computer science, and commerce, respectively. The biggest surprise may be that American English accounts for almost half of the new words and meanings added.

Chapter 2

One of nature's mistakes is the birth of twins whose bodies are joined together. Such twins are called Siamese twins because the most famous pair of united twins was born in Siam. Siamese twins result when a single fertilized ovum begins to separate into two embryos, but the separation is not complete. The result is identical twins who are united in some part of the body, such as the chest, the back, or the head. Siamese twins are relatively rare. Only four or five pairs are born in the world each year. However, most of them die at birth or soon after because Siamese twins characteristically have many physical problems. Now and then a pair survives, and some pairs have been successfully separated into two individuals. Before separation can be attempted, however, doctors must determine if the twins share important body parts. If separation by surgery might result in the death of one or both twins, surgery is usually not attempted. Instead, the twins remain united for life in the most intimate relationship possible.

Chapter 3

The length of the day and year is based on the movement of the earth, but the movement of the earth is unpredictable. Because the earth rotates irregularly and actually wobbles on its axis, it eventually gets out of synchronization with time. To overcome this problem, a system using space technology was devised to measure changes in the earth's rotation and speed. Evolving from this system is the use of leap seconds that are added or subtracted to keep time accurately. On December 31, 1987, a leap second was added to the last minute of the year. The previous addition was made two and a half years before. Without these extra seconds, time would drift along and we would ultimately have clocks that are too fast or too slow.

Chapter 4

Before Stephen Wozniak and Steven Jobs introduced the personal computer, they had already demonstrated their technological potential. They had built and sold a blue box, which was a pocket-sized device that allowed telephone users to make long-distance calls for free. Although Wozniak insists that he never used the illegally devised blue box to defraud the telephone company, he boasted about using the invention to call the Vatican and get through to Pope Paul VI. Soon after the blue box was devised, it was discovered and banned.

Chapter 5

Radio was still a new narrative medium in 1938. Perhaps this explains why American radio listeners so easily believed "War of the Worlds," a radio drama about a spaceship landing in an eastern town. At the beginning of the program, the radio announcer revealed that the narrative to follow was a dramatization of an H. G. Wells literary classic. Yet listeners seemed to forget that announcement a few minutes later when live orchestra music was interrupted by a news report of a spaceship landing. The illusion of reality was maintained by returning to the music and interrupting it from time to time with a sequence of news reports that conveyed dramatic details of the attack by visitors from space. This narrative technique was so effective that it literally created panic near the town where the spaceship in the story had landed. Radio listeners had visions of being attacked by spacemen, and the situation seemed critical. Without thinking coherently, people left their homes to hide from the dangers they visualized. Hours later they returned home feeling a little foolish when they realized they had reacted to a radio version of a famous science fiction story.

Chapter 6

Most Americans are first introduced to junk food when they are young children. Junk food is often named and packaged in a way that will attract a child's attention. One hour of children's television programming contains as many as 20 commercials for highly sweetened and processed food products that attract young eaters. Young children thereby learn to accept sugar, sweetness, and chocolate as fundamental components of a normal diet. If parents want to enforce dietary rules in their homes, they have to isolate their children from the influences of these advertisements or somehow convince the children to be selective about the foods they eat.

Chapter 7

A nonprofit organization called Helping Hands has fought to accommodate the needs of quadriplegics. This innovative group trains small monkeys so they can meet a myriad of the small but significant needs that a severely disabled person faces every day. A monkey named Jo, for example, has become proficient at a broad scope of commonplace tasks that include bringing books or magazines, bringing drinks from the refrigerator, clearing away empty glasses, and picking up dropped items. The more Jo is exposed to her responsibilities, the more she seems to learn. She is able to respond to audible commands such as bring or change. She can also respond to visual cues from a small light that her master uses to point out articles he wants her to bring. Jo's master won't deny that there is an occasional misunderstanding between himself and his little companion, but she has enabled him to avoid an enormous number of exhausting tasks, and therefore she deserves a lot of credit.

Chapter 8

During the winter of 1989, the sparsely inhabited state of Alaska endured one of the most intense cold waves ever to strike this northern area. Although the weather in Alaska is always intensely cold in the winter, warm ocean winds usually help raise the temperatures somewhat. In 1989, however, a high-pressure mass of cold air from the north settled in the path of the fickle ocean winds and prevented them from reaching Alaska. This strong high-pressure system was responsible for temperatures as low as −75 °F. High-velocity winds intensified the effects of the cold wave and generated tremendous snow storms. The storms paralyzed the state. Schools and businesses closed, and transportation was disrupted. Heating gas liquified, and steel equipment froze and cracked into pieces. When the storm finally blew into Canada, Alaska's inhabitants were glad to see it go.

GLOSSARY

Adjective: modifies or describes nouns and specifies size, color, number, and other characteristics.

*Three **big, black, fuzzy** bears crawled from the **dark** cave.*

Adverb: describes verbs, adjectives, and other adverbs. They specify in what manner, when, where, and how much.

***Yesterday** the stock prices went up **very rapidly**.*

Adverbial: a word or word group that modifies or changes the meaning of other words, phrases, clauses, or sentences.

*Lyman collided with another skier, but **fortunately** was hurt **hardly at all**.*

Clause: a group of words that has a subject and a verb combination in it. An independent clause may be a complete sentence or part of a longer sentence. A dependent clause is not a complete sentence and must be combined with an independent clause.

The computer has changed our lives. (independent clause)
Since it was invented (dependent clause), the computer has been greatly improved (independent clause).

Colloquialism: word or term that is characteristic of conversation and informal writing.

*I took my **kid** to the dentist.*

Comparative: word forms or word groups that compare or contrast two persons, things, or groups. (See Superlative)

*My nose is **bigger than** my brother's nose.*
*My English professor is **more interesting than** my chemistry professor.*
*I work **as hard as** my boss does.*

Intransitive verb: a verb that does not require a noun object to follow. (See Transitive verb)

$$\text{S} \qquad \text{V}$$
*The dog **barked** constantly.*

Noun:

A **common noun** refers to a person, place, or thing.

> *child*   *school*   *book*   *knowledge*

A **proper noun** refers to a particular person, place, or thing.

> *Noah Webster*   *Washington, D.C.*   *the Civil War*

A **count noun** refers to something that can be counted.

> *a student/10 students*   *a year/100 years*

A **non-count noun** refers to something that cannot be counted.

> *bread/some bread*   *steel/some steel*   *darkness*   *clothing*

Object (O): tells who or what received the action of the main verb in a sentence.

*Hernando Cortez conquered **Mexico**.*

Participle: either of two verb forms (present participle ending in -ing, or past participle ending in -ed) that may be used in a verb phrase or as an adjective. Some past participles are irregular. (See verbs)

*The fire was **burning**.*
*The trees were **burned**.*
*The **burning** fire was out of control.*
*Only **burned** trees remained.*

Passive: a form of a transitive verb in which the subject receives the action.

>   S   V   O
> Active form: *The fire destroyed the forest.*

>   O   V   S
> Passive form: *The forest **was destroyed** by the fire.*

By + ***an agent*** (what or who did the action) may be omitted if the agent is unknown or unimportant: *The forest was destroyed.*

Phrase: two or more words that work as a unit within a clause or sentence.

***While studying**, John was interrupted **by a phone call**.*

Preposition: shows the relationship in time and space between ideas.

*David parked his Volvo **by** the bicycle **in** the garage.*

Subject: (S): who or what the speaker is talking about in a sentence.

*Sad **movies** make Linda cry.*

Superlative: used in comparison or contrast when one person or thing is different from the others in a group. (See Comparative)

> Her dog is **the friendliest** in our neigborhood.
> English is **the most difficult** language I have studied.
> Math is **the least interesting** course that I take.

Transitive verb: must be followed by a noun object. (See Intransitive verb)

> S   V   O
> The dog **chewed** the shoe.

Two-word verb: formed from a verb and a preposition or an adverb. A two-word verb functions as a unit.

> Please **fill out** this form. (Please **complete** this form.)
> We **get up** early. (We **arise** early.)

Verb (v): shows action or a state of being. Some verbs have irregular past tense and past participle forms such as eat/ate/eaten.

> I **waited** at the bus terminal for two hours.
> I **am** tired.

VOCABULARY LIST

Page numbers refer to words as they appear in an article or word form chart. Numbers in bold refer to explanations of the words.

flourish 161
focus 96
foresee 73, **88**
foreseeable 85
foreseeably 85
foreseen 85
foresight 85
form (noun) 3
form (verb) 4
formation 15
formative 15
formerly 122
formulate 18
fraternal 26
fundamental 122

gadget 75
gene 25
generate 165, **167**
generic 4, **14**
genetically 26
genuine 75

habitat **176**
habitation **176**
handicapped 142
heir 46
hereditary 37
heredity 25
heritage **46**

identical 26
illiteracy **117**
illiterate **117**
illusion 97
immobile 142
immobility 151
immobilization 151
immobilize **156**
impact 4
inaccuracy 52
inconclusive 37
inconclusively 37
inconsistency 2
indestructible 175
indigestible 122
indistinguishable 26
individual (adj.) 37

individual (noun) 25
individualization 37
individualize 37
individually 13
inequitable 125
inevitable 77
influence 28, **31**
ingenuity 125, **130**
inhabit 161
inhabitable 175
inhabitant 175
inherent 25
inherently **45**
inherit 37
inheritance 37
inherited 37
innovate 85
innovation 73
innovative 85
innovativeness 85
innovator 73
intense **183**
intensely **183**
intensification **183**
intensify **183**
intensity 164, **183**
intensive **183**
intensively **183**
integrated circuit 75
interrelated **39**
interrelationship 37
intimidate 73
intimidating 85
intimidation 85
inundate 51, **67**
inundation **67**
investment 77
invisible 161
invisibly 161
irresistible **178**
isolate 123

leap year 52, **59**
literacy **117**
literal **117**
literally 96
literary **117**

literate **117**
literature **117**
live (adj.) 95
located 163
lunar 52

makeshift 75
market (noun) 76, **86**
market (verb) 85
marketable 85
marketablity 85
marketing 85
massive 73
medium 94
microprocessor 75
mobile **155**
mobility **155**
mobilization **156**
mobilize **156**
moderation 122
moist 164
monitor 143, **149**
mood 97
multilingual 3
muted 76
myriad 144

narrative 94
nonexistence **136**
nonexistent **136**
nourish 121

observable 63
observance 67
observant 63
observation 63
observe 52, **67**
observing 63
occupation 2
occupied 15
occupy 15
origin 175
original 175
originally 175
originate 164, **167**
origination 175
originator 175
ova 26

overcome   52
ovum   29

paralysis   151
paralyze   142, **156**
paralyzing   151
paraplegic   142
partially   2
passionately   76
path   164
perform   96, **102**
peripherals   76
personality   27
phases   52
phenomenon   25
physical   27
physique   26
pioneer   75
plot   96
popular   95, **115**
popularity   107
popularize   107
popularly   107
potential   73
practical   51
precise   51
predict   51, **65**
predictable   **66**
predictably   **66**
prediction   **65**
predominance   15
predominant   15
predominantly   15
predominate   17
pregnancy   26
preoccupation   121
preoccupied   15
pressure   163
prevent   165, **169**
preventable   175
prevention   175
preventive   175
previous   53
processed   124
produce   124
producer   131
production   131

productive   131
proficient   143
progress (noun)   **19**
progress (verb)   1
progressive   **20**
progressively   **19**
project   96
prolong   142
prominence   124
prompt   51
prospect   144
protein   122
provide   165, **180, 181**
provided (that)   **181**
provision   175
provisionally   175
psychological   28
pursue   131, **138**
pursuing   131
pursuit   121, **138**

quadriplegic   141

realize   95
rear   27, **33**
recognition   52, **69**
recognizable   63
recognizably   63
recognize   **69**
recognizing   63
reflect   1, **20**
reflection   15
reflective   21
reflectively   15
reform   4
regard (noun)   63
regard (verb)   **66**
regardless of   **66**
regardlessly   63
related   37, **39**
relation   37
relationship   26
relative (noun)   **40**
relative (adj.)   **40**
relatively   **40**
renovations   142
represent   21

representation   21
representative (noun)   21
representative (adj.)   21
resemble   25
resist   **178**
resistance   **178**
resistant   163, **178**
respectively   3
resource   **129**
resourceful   124
resourcefully   132
resourcefulness   **129**
responsible (for)   165, **169**
result (noun)   37, **43**
result (verb)   26
resulting   37
reunited   27
reveal   97
revolutionize   97
rhythmic   52
richness   2, **12**
role   25
rotating   164
roughly   52

scene   95
scope   142
screen   94
selective   123
self-sufficient   144
sensation   95, **107**
sensational   **107**
sensationally   107
sense (noun)   **108**
sense (verb)   **107**
sensitive   **108**
sensitively   107
sensitivity   107
separate (verb)   26
sequence   95
severely   142
sibling   26
significance   54
similar   27
simultaneously   94
skeptical   76